I'm on the Right Road Now

I'm on the Right Road Now

• • •

Marc L. Nichols

ISBN-13: 9781534625884
ISBN-10: 1534625887
Library of Congress Control Number: 2016909661
CreateSpace Independent Publishing Platform
North Charleston, South Carolina

Preface

● ● ●

THE DAY MY FATHER PASSED, I began to write down the short stories that I have told all my life to friends and family members, and I started posting them to Facebook. It started out as a way to share *funny* stories that I could remember about my father, and I hoped it would make me and other family members smile through some of the upcoming tough days. I had a host of encouraging comments from my family and friends who sent private messages on Facebook, expressing how much they enjoyed the stories. Others sent text messages, and some called to tell me that the stories kept them laughing most of the day or even just brightened their day. Some asked me to continue to tell more stories and embarrass myself with more stories of whoopins, and others suggested I write a book made up of these short stories.

But there was one person (as there always is) who asked me why—*why* would I put all my business on Facebook and share with the world (most being strangers) such intimate details of my life? I couldn't answer the question at the time; I just didn't know the answer! Then one night, during my evening workout (which consisted of jogging three miles and lifting weights), I had an opportunity to "marinate" on that question. "Why would I share the intimate details of my life on Facebook?"—and just like that, my epiphany was born:

* I liken it to a child who rises on Christmas Day and can't help but show his or her joy for gifts.
* I liken it to a teenager who has accomplished twelve years of school and is about to take that final walk across the stage.

- I liken it to someone who is out of work; bills are due, and he or she gets the call with a job offer.
- I liken it to a parent who has watched kids all day and finally gets a break with adult interaction.
- I liken it to someone who has had a long workweek, and it's finally Friday—time for *happy hour.*
- I liken it to someone who has had a spiritual awakening and has seen the light with regard to his or her salvation.

My *entire life* has been a testimony of what God has done for me. The peaks, the valleys, the hurdles, and my failures and successes through them all have helped shape and mold my life today. When something good happens in your life, you have to *tell* somebody—you have to *share* it with someone because you never know whom you might encourage, inspire, or motivate! I shared my "lessons" because I couldn't keep them to myself!

Prologue

• • •

BISHOP LUKE COTTON NICHOLS WAS born November 26, 1927, in Chicago, Illinois, to SilKirtus and Adglee Nichols, and he was the oldest of five children. He attributed his moral discipline to receiving a Mississippi/Arkansas upbringing in the city of Chicago; his father was from Mississippi, his mother from Arkansas. As a young man, my father grew up during the Great Depression, and he had no problem explaining how many nights he and his family went to bed hungry or that the only thing they had to eat was onion soup. I could tell that it adversely affected my father by the amount of food he ate and his eating our food if we failed to clean our plates. A couple of his favorite sayings were "Waste not, want not" and "If you get hungry enough, you will eat anything."

My paternal grandfather was a minister/pastor at the same church that my father eventually came to pastor. My grandfather decided to leave the city of Chicago, following God's orders that he should pastor in the city of Omaha, Nebraska. At the time, my father and his two siblings were unaware of the move. The plan was for my grandfather to move and then send for the rest of the family. However, my grandmother was not fond of the idea of leaving her life and family in Chicago and decided that she would not move. For years, my father and his siblings believed that he had abandoned them.

My parents met and soon married, and to this union they added seven children: four boys and three girls. After my mother's death in 1977, my father remarried and adopted his new wife's two children, a boy and girl, totaling nine altogether.

My father was a minister for as long as I can remember. But he wasn't just a pastor of a church—he was also a truck driver, and he worked at the Omaha Public Housing Authority. In those days, pastors/ministers had to have additional income to help make ends meet. My father also spent most of his time giving and ministering to others while on his Christian journey through life. He either organized or participated in many of the Christian organizations to help in the community or to fight against poverty and even police brutality. He allowed the local Boy Scout troop to utilize the church as a meeting place, and he was often on the radio or television in Omaha on KETV, promoting the Christian way of life and preaching on an hour-long Sunday morning program. I can still hear him saying the famous words: "Come on down to 2029 Binney," which is the address for the Church of the Living God.

When I was a young boy of about six or seven years of age, I often put on one of my father's large shirts, stood behind the coffee table, and preached to my mother and baby sister. I could always envision him in the pulpit, yelling at the top of his lungs, trying to teach the masses. Oftentimes, he walked around the church with no microphone and only his authoritative, deep, booming voice.

They say that imitation is the sincerest form of flattery, and I found myself imitating my father then and, on certain occasions, even now!

My father's first home was the church. Before my mother passed, he never had to worry too much about the duties of the family home. My mother didn't work outside the home, but she ran a small daycare inside the house to help make ends meet. I remember accompanying my father to the church many days. We were the first to arrive to unlock the doors and the last to depart, making sure the doors were secured. After my mother passed, my father continued his duties, not only at the church, but also in the home. He couldn't boil water, wash or fold clothes, vacuum, wash dishes, or even mop. Men of that era were not accustomed to doing household chores. His seven children took care of all the manual labor around the house. I watched as he struggled to learn the basics from my older sisters; they were getting older, and their time in the home was becoming short. My father recognized it, and during times that we rode alone in the car, he often mentioned to me that I needed to learn how to perform these tasks so that I could live on my own. My father eventually learned to boil water, cook, and clean and fold clothes. He had become a man of many talents in the home, extending beyond his minister/pastor role. I had watched the transformation, and I was expected to do the same.

This book of short stories is based on my interactions with my father for forty-plus years. It was not an easy road—often rocky, tumultuous, and filled with a lot of pain. I have attempted to write these stories to pay tribute to my father by showing how he lived his life and the kind of man he was. I am hopeful that the stories will give some insight into both of our lives and reveal some of the lessons that I learned along the way to pass on to my children, grandchildren, nephews, nieces, and anyone else who is willing to listen and learn.

CHAPTER 1

Sibling Rivalry

● ● ●

SO IT HAD TO BE about 1974, and my old man was the pastor of the Church of the Living God, 2029 Binney Street, District Number Seven, Temple No. Thirty-Three. Every so often, he was also invited to go to another church within the "brotherhood" to preach. This Sunday, my father was requested to have church in Topeka, Kansas, for the day. The entire congregation was to meet at our church in Omaha and travel together to Topeka for the day.

We had a brown Plymouth station wagon with the third-row seat that faced the rear of the car. Those who rode in that third seat (normally my sister and I) faced the people following us. The station wagons back in those days came equipped with a door that was similar to a pickup truck's tailgate, which opened on a hinge like a regular car door. In our car, my mother and father sat in the front seat, my two older sisters and our ever-faithful rider/choir director sat in the second seat, and last, but not least, my younger sister and I sat in the third seat. As we rolled along, we began fighting and, as *usual*, I was getting the best of her. My father yelled back at me in that deep voice that he used, "Marc, I done told you to sit down and shut it up!"

Now me being *me*, I called out, "She hit me first!"

"I don't care what she did—don't you hit her no more!"

As soon as he turned his head, I let her have it again! *Why?* Heck, I don't know!

So the old man pulled over to the side of the road. He was *hot* as fish grease, because not only had I done pushed him to the limit, but I had also hit his youngest girl. He got out of the car, moved to the rear of the vehicle, and opened the rear door. So again, me being *me*, I jumped to the second seat when he got to the

1

back of the station wagon. He went up to the side door, and I jumped back to the third seat again. He then stopped and said, "You move one more time if you want to—*I dare you*! If you move one more time, I'm gonna stomp a mud hole in your behind and walk it dry!" (It was his favorite threat; I didn't understand that line until I became a man—and that's a lot of stompin'!) So he finally got at me and *boy, oh boy*—he snatched me out of that third-row seat and onto the shoulder of the highway. My father wore a double-pronged belt that was made of real leather; it was thick and heavy, and he happened to be very "proficient" with it. When he got me, I was in the middle of trying to make my move back to the second seat of the car, and he caught me by my ankles. Before I knew it, I was in his grasp, hanging upside down. As I was squirming in his grasp, I could see him taking off his belt with one hand and grabbing the other end *while* still holding me by my ankles. Once I got my bearings, I could see—even upside down—that the *entire* congregation had also pulled over and was watching "the show" of my father teaching me one of those valuable lessons, and I have not lived that event down to this day!

But looking back, all I can do is laugh and say what a blessing it is to have someone *teach* you that there are consequences to your actions.

#FinallyLearnedtheLesson

CHAPTER 2

Public Housing Authority

● ● ●

IT TOOK MY OLDER SISTER to remind me how tight my father and I were at one time; I was always trying to mimic him, and I followed him *everywhere* he went. One summer, I asked my father if I could go to work with him, and this was one of those *very* rare times that he allowed me to accompany him. At this time—I can't remember my exact age—but my father worked at the Omaha Housing Authority (better known as the projects). He worked with displaced or underprivileged families to aid them in getting adequate or affordable housing based on their income. For those who lived in Omaha at that time, I believe it was the Hilltop Projects, located at about Thirtieth and Lake Streets (where a Walgreens and Salem Baptist Church sit now).

At that time, my father had a fairly new vehicle. He pampered his vehicle and made certain that it was never dirty; if it got dirty, it wasn't for long. This man actually washed his car while it was raining. I even observed him wash his car in the winter with salt on the ground and a storm brewing. He always said that he couldn't ride to the house of the Lord in a dirty machine (or "'chine," as he called it).

So, he allowed me to accompany him to work that day. My father shared his office with another individual, and the room wasn't very large (it was a little tight in there). But, there was a big window facing the parking lot. Now in the projects there was always something going on: people congregated in the common areas or kids played football or kickball. While my father was busy doing paperwork, I noticed a man (maybe twenty-two or twenty-three years of age) sitting on my dad's car—which I *knew* was a no-no in our house. So me being *me*, I turned to my father and said, "Dad, there's a man outside sitting on your car!" (You could almost hear the record-scratch sound when he looked up from those documents.)

I followed my father outside as he confronted the man. My father said, "Excuse me, son, you're sitting on my automobile."

He looked up at my dad and said, "It's only a car, man."

My dad responded, "Yes, but it's *my* car!" The dude jumped off the car, continued to talk to his buddies, and we returned to the office.

Maybe twenty minutes later, I observed the *same* dude sitting on my father's car again. Although I knew I shouldn't—yeah, I was a tattle-tale (my older brothers stopped taking me places because I would tell my mother, and then she would give them the fifth degree)—but I said, "*Daaaaaadyyyyyyy*, that man is sitting on your car again!" You could see the frustration on my father's face, and he stormed out of the office to confront this man again. So you *know* I was right behind him waiting to see the "show"! My father approached the man, for the second time, and asked him not to sit on his car. He said he didn't like having to come out and tell him to get off his 'chine (short for machine)!

Dude said, "It's only a car, old man!" and that was it—my father grabbed that dude off the hood of his car and gave him a few quick jabs! And when he was done, he picked him up, dusted him off, and said if he had to come back out there again, he wouldn't be as nice.

I always saw my father as a big, tough guy who could handle himself and *not* just as a preacher after that day. He showed me how to confront someone by using communication skills and conflict resolution. He also showed me how to *value* what you have worked hard for, but not worship it or allow it to control you. I *love* a nice ride and nice things, and I work hard to obtain them. That lesson also taught me that there will be times when you have to respond in-kind when some may push you to your limit, and that being *Crist*-like is a daily walk, but everyone falls short.

#FinallyLearnedtheLesson

CHAPTER 3

Spectator

• • •

BACK IN THE DAY, I was a rambunctious, all-American, red-blooded boy. I was mischievous, hardheaded, and what some would classify as athletic. Because of my father's occupation, my mother's illness, and my brothers' off living their lives with their families, I didn't have much guidance or "structure" outside the confines of the church.

We lived at 4210 North Thirty-Sixth Street, two houses away from one of the oldest high schools in North Omaha (North High School), and it was a great community. Back then, we rarely closed doors, let alone locked them. I can remember almost all our neighbors from back then, including their children, some of whom were old enough to be MY parents. The Dunbars (who lived right next door to our home) were an older couple who had several kids. One of their sons was a coach for a local football team called the Swazzers, or Lil' Red Machine. I saw Mr. Dunbar on occasion when he visited his parents. He drove an older truck that he oftentimes filled with football equipment.

I ran wild in the neighborhood back in the day, and we routinely met down on the boulevard and play football with all the neighborhood kids. We even had our own neighborhood football team that went from neighborhood to neighborhood, playing football (one of the ways we met other kids from different parts of the city and began to build bonds or friendships outside our neighborhood). One day Mr. Dunbar observed some of us kids playing football and asked if I would like to play "real" football. I looked at him, and he could probably see in my expression that I was thinking, yeah dude—I'm already playing "real" football. He chuckled, and then stated, "With pads and everything." I was about nine at the time and had never played in pads; I had only witnessed my older brother play for North High.

I always had a fascination with the game and those who played; I could tell you from a young age who all the Dallas Cowboys and Chicago Bears players were. I can recall in my early years being so enthralled with the game, and I knew where to go to watch—my second-oldest brother went to North High School. My mother was a child care provider at that time and had her hands full most mornings with children being dropped off, so it was easy for me to slip away. I routinely sneaked out of the house via the back door, exit our property through the driveway, take a left, go up the hill about three houses, cross the street, stand up against the ten-foot fence, and watch the team practice. (Years later as a teenager, I would jump that fence to play on the football field of what I thought would be my future school.) Back then, North had two practices—one before school, and the other after. My brother was on the team along with all his friends from the neighborhood, and they would eventually see me standing there half-naked, with no shoes on, and probably yelling their names. My brother would jump the fence in full gear and take me home, fussin' at me the entire way. "Momma, he was up at the school again. You have to keep a better eye on him!" Some days, she would even walk me up the street, and we would watch the practice together…

Mr. Dunbar began to pick me up for practice and drop me off every day. In those days, we practiced at Green Hill or Adams Park. I was a young guy, so playing was not in the cards for me at that time. I can recall riding my bike to the park for practice on several occasions. I was dropped off back at the park before and after the games. On my way home, I would jump off my bike and roll in the dirt so that it looked like I had played in the games. My parents didn't come to practice or the games; they were busy working or ministering to others' needs in the community.

I can recall having a game at Dodge Park in about 1976 or so. Again, I was younger and not getting in the games. (Later on in life, I found out that kids who didn't have support were often overlooked because there was no one there to speak on their behalf.) So I spent a lot of time walking the sidelines and watching the crowd. I looked up once and saw a familiar car sitting on the side of the road. I would recognize that station wagon anywhere. My mother and father were observing the game from the parked car. My mother was very ill at that time and could not do much, and I can imagine that sitting in the car, watching the game, took about all the strength she could muster. I don't recall my parent(s) coming to another game; although, my father told me that he attended my last game in high school (some eleven years later) and watched me take the field for the final time at Shawnee High School in 1985.

I'd like to thank Mr. Dunbar for many things: noticing me that day playing in the yard, being a community leader, and having compassion for his neighbors—who he could probably tell were going through a rough time in life. He was also a shining example of what *God* has called us all to be to those who are less fortunate or haven't found their way. I have never forgotten his acts of kindness, and I always knew that he played a very important role in my "coaching" life!

As I look back over the mountains and the valleys of life and the way I harbored those feelings of "abandonment," I realize that learned a few lessons that directly affected my children and me as they pertain to sports and father/child relationships:

* I always wanted a father who would be supportive with respect to sports. I thought if my parent was more involved, I could learn so much more and be productive.
* I always wanted a cheering section like the one my friends had. One of my sisters (of six siblings) was supportive and attended track meets and football games when she could.
* Most times, I was the kid with no support, which certainly helped shape and mold me into the person that I have become.
* I learned that I became the father that I always wanted. I coached my children since birth and always took part in their extracurricular activities, homework, and presentations. I also performed chaperone duties.

My father taught me many direct and indirect lessons on my journey through life. One of the most important lessons I learned was that I can't go back and rewrite my past, for my past has made me who I am today; however, I can "pen" my own future. I also learned that I could *be* the father I've always wanted to be to my children in an effort to break the cycle and help my children and their children live life more abundantly.

#FinallyLearnedtheLesson

CHAPTER 4

The Deuce

● ● ●

I CAME DOWN THE HILL going as fast as possible, pulling into the driveway, and skidding to a halt when I saw my mother and my maternal grandmother, known as "Mother"—she did not like to be called Grandmother—standing in the driveway. Both greeted me with yelling and purses swinging!

Earlier in the day, my friends and I decided to leave the boulevard and head down to the Deuce. The Deuce, short for Twenty-Fourth Street, was the most popular street in North Omaha where you could shop, get a haircut, play ball, eat at soul food restaurants and popular BBQ joints, buy snacks and soda at drug stores, and find assisted-living quarters and the black-owned funeral parlors. Back in the day, it was as crowded as the New York City streets you'd see on television commercials. You could see mothers walking hand-in-hand with their children, men entering and exiting the various barbershops, churches on nearly every corner, as well as full-service gas stations (some open for business and others the front for the local crap house) that were equipped to sell gas or provide mechanical service. From Twenty-Fourth and Ames to Twenty-Fourth and Cuming (about a four-mile stretch), you were sure to see and hear it all. The Deuce was also known for liquor stores, nightclubs, and available women of the night during hours of darkness.

The year was 1975, and I was eight years old. My friends and I decided to head down to the Deuce to see what was going on—maybe swing by the Kellom projects, play some neighborhood football. We might get a burger at McDonald's on the corner of Twenty-Fourth and Cuming (Cuming could be the beginning or end of the Deuce, depending on which direction you were traveling), and then head back to the neighborhood. I was brought up in a strict home; we weren't allowed to listen to secular music in the house, play cards, and my father certainly wasn't too fond of board games. He would let you know that his house was God's dwelling and not a house of ill repute. So my friends and I left the boulevard and headed down to the Deuce. We rode down Sprague Street, crossing over Thirtieth Street and on to the Deuce. We took a right and rode the entire length of Twenty-Fourth Street down to Hamilton Street into the projects, where we played some football, then headed to McDonald's to get burgers, sit on our bikes, and people watch.

My mother was yelling at me, asking what I had been doing and where I was. Back then, I wouldn't hesitate to *lie* to my mother to cover up where I had been. I was nine years old, and I knew that I was not allowed to go past the immediate area; I was very fortunate to be able to leave the block! Finally, my mother calmed down enough to talk, but my grandmother was standing behind her, acting as her cheerleader. My mother asked me again, "Where have you been?"

I said, "On the boulevard, riding my bike."

"That's funny," my mother responded. "Sista King said she saw you down on Twenty-Fourth Street, cussin'!"

DEAD SILENCE

Sister King was one of the missionaries of the church. Every day, before and after school, my mother picked up my sister and me at Sister King's house Do to her close proximity to Saratoga Elementary School allowed us to walk to and from school. So make no mistake—she knew who I was, and if she said she saw me—she saw me—and that was the end of the story! My mother asked me again, "Marc, were you down on Twenty-Fourth Street?"

"No, ma'am," I replied.

SILENCE "

So Sista King is a liar?"

THINKING

I replied, "No ma'am."

She then asked, "Which is it—were you on Twenty-Fourth Street cussin', or is Sista King a liar?" My mother had been ill and didn't have a lot of strength to deal with me or punish me in the manner in which she was accustomed.

My mother had been a big disciplinarian in the past. She had no issue with grabbing whatever was handy—from an extension cord, iron, or a racecar track—or she would have us go get a switch. I can remember many a day my mother chased me throughout the house. One time I was going to "run away." I got a small bag and headed around the corner to one of the church member's homes over on Thirty-Seventh Street. After playing all day and seeing that the streetlights were slowly flickering and beginning to come on, one of the boys said that I should head home (they were older and knew the rules in the hood). I confided in them my plan not to return home. After a long talk with them, they finally convinced me to return home and even agreed to walk with me to the house. What I hadn't known was their mother called my mother to inform her where I was and that the boys were accompanying me to the house.

Once home, my mother instructed me to eat and get ready for bed (which included taking a bath in her room). I finished eating, ran my bathwater, gathered my belongings from my room, and returned to jump in the tub. Many of you may remember the "skeleton key" that was used for doors in older homes. My parents had one of these keys; however, it was not in the door when I reached to lock the door. I didn't think anything of it at the time, and jumped into the tub and began to play with my Hot Wheels (yes, I played with Hot wheels in the tub). Suddenly the door opened, and my mother stood in the doorway, holding an orange racecar track. She got a chair, sat on the side of the tub, and began to question me about my feeble attempt to run away. I told her that I wasn't really running away, and she replied, "I know!" Before I knew it, she was using that racecar track to teach me a lesson I will never forget. I was sorry I even thought about running away after that "misunderstanding..."

"I'm waiting for the answer!" Now I could say that Sista King was a liar, or I could tell the truth—either way, there would *not* be a positive outcome for me. My mother was winded just talking to me at this point, and my grandmother was chomping at the bit to get at me. But because she was older now as well, they thought it best to wait for my father to return home. I put my bike away and went to my room to await the inevitable. My room faced the driveway, so I would immediately see any car that went past, stopped, or pulled into the driveway.

Any one of the siblings who got into trouble—and we knew was going to "get it"—would be badgered until the moment of truth arrived. My sisters would stand outside my room taunting me by saying, "Doom-de-doom-doom...

doom-de-doom-doom-*dooooooommmm*" (the music that all movies had back then whenever death or destruction was certain)! My father was also known for his beat-downs and gave no mercy when pushed to the limit—and it seemed as if I was always pushing the limits.

Well, the moment had arrived; I saw the headlights to the station wagon pull into the driveway, and my father got out of the car and entered the house. I stood outside my room and listened to the conversation. When he entered the house, my mother immediately called out, "LC!" (Everyone who knew my father from back in the day called him by his initials.) She told him the story about me being on Twenty-Fourth Street and cussing, and that he needed to go upstairs and do something because she just couldn't do it any longer! My father meandered around the house, and finally, an hour or so later, he came into my room.

My father came into my room visibly tired, sat on the edge of my bed, and began to speak to me. He asked where I was on Twenty-Fourth Street. I told him on Twenty-Fourth and Hamilton in front of the Bali Hi (which was a nightclub/lounge). He asked what I was doing down there, and I explained that my friends and I rode our bikes to the Kellom Housing Projects to play them in football. Then we went to McDonald's and had a burger, and then we were talking with friends outside the Bali Hi. My father explained that he was tired and didn't have time to put it on me (as he put it). He said that I was too young to be that far away and that people would see everything I did and report back to my parents—so I couldn't get away with much. He finally said that I was a representative of my mother and father, and how I acted in public said a lot about them as parents.

I didn't get a whoopin' that night; he tore me down and built me back up again with nothing but words, and it didn't feel good. I learned that evening that the true character of a man is determined by what he does and says when no one is watching. I will never forget that night my father came home and just talked to me. The words he spoke that night rang loud in my ears for years to follow.

#FinallyLearnedtheLesson

CHAPTER 5

Taking Responsibility

● ● ●

IT WAS 1976, AND I was about nine years old. Just like any other young child, I listened and learned a lot from my parents through their conversations with one another. It was a Sunday evening and, as always, my father was watching Lawrence Welk in the living room. My mother was in her room, which was off the dining room and situated behind the living room. At that age, I wanted to do everything my father did. So as he sat in his La-Z-Boy chair, I sat on the couch watching Lawrence Welk with him. The phone rang, and my mother called my father into the room for a short conversation. My father exited, and then returned to the living room without saying a word. My mother exited her room shortly after, with her hat and shoes on and her purse draped over her arm.

All my life, my father made and enforced the rules of the home. He was a heavy-handed and stern disciplinarian and knew how to tell a story or use his physical strength to get his point across.

One Saturday afternoon, all the kids were home and a fight broke out. Did I mention that my parents had seven kids—four boys and three girls—with about eighteen years between the oldest and the youngest? On this day, my three older brothers got into a free-for-all (just like in a western); it started upstairs, and ended up on the main floor. They managed to break the banister that led from the top floor to the main floor, the screen door, and, I believe, the coffee table. My sister called the church where both my parents were doing whatever it is they did.

My father and mother arrived in two separate cars—my father in a VW Bug and my mother in the family station wagon. My three sisters and I were sitting on the front porch watching the festivities. My father parked on the street, while my mother pulled into the driveway. My dad scurried up the walkway and the porch stairs (the four of us move quickly out of his way) and into the house. My mother ushered us off to the side, but, as she was getting the "story" from my sisters, I managed to follow behind my father to see what exactly was going on. When I rounded the corner, I saw my father with two of my brothers (the second- and third-oldest) as he had them pent up against the wall, yelling at them. I don't remember the words, but it was something to the effect of this being his *home! My oldest brother ran out of the house while my father was preoccupied and ran up the street (we didn't see him for a while)...*

As my mother began to exit the home and my father and I continued to watch Lawrence Welk, they had a very interesting exchange that I will *never* forget:

FATHER: "Shirley, where are you going?"
MOTHER: "I'm going down to get him."
FATHER: "I told you that we are not going to get him out."
MOTHER: "LC, I can't leave him down there."
FATHER: "I'm not gonna tell you again that we are not going to bail him out; he has to learn the consequences of his actions."
MOTHER: "It's the group he is hanging with—they're the wrong crowd and influencing him!"

LONG PAUSE

Now my father was one of the realest people I've ever met—he minced no words and found a way to say what he meant whether you liked it or not. In that *deep* voice, and without looking away from the TV, my father said something that I have *never* forgotten in over forty years:

FATHER: "Shirley, *he is* the wrong crowd! And if you leave this house, I don't know where you're going to go, but neither of you will set foot back here at forty-two ten!"

My father had laid down the law, and my mother turned from the door and went back to her room without as much as another word. One of my brothers had evidently done something to get himself locked up. Although I don't know what he did, my father didn't believe that he was innocent or that he had the obligation to bail him out; he would have to sit in jail and deal with the consequences of his actions. Even at such an early age, that exchange taught me some very deep life lessons that have served me well throughout my adult life:

- There needs to be and should be a *balance*—children have to be taught that there are consequences for their actions and that you have to be willing to accept the punishment for unlawful behavior.
- If you don't know whom you're dealing with, look at his or her friends, and that will certainly tell you a lot about the person.
- Being a man of principle means that sometimes you have to make the tough calls and stand on said principles—*even* when others disagree.
- Tough love sometimes means *not* lending a hand so that those who fall are asking for a hand up and not a handout and make changes for the better.

My father taught me that day that *if I so choose* to be on the opposite side of the law that he would *not* be there to hold my hand, call in favors, put money on my books, or talk to the judge. He made it clear that he would say a prayer that I learn from my mistakes and that God continue to watch over me on my journey. My father also taught me that being a father may sometimes mean that you must allow your children to fall in order for them to learn *their own lessons*. I have *never* done a day in jail, never had handcuffs on my wrists, and I thank God for being allowed to hear that conversation on that evening and for the explanation that was given. I *never* wanted to be "the wrong crowd"!

On several occasions I have talked to my own children about consequences for their actions, and each time that subject is broached, I think of that Sunday afternoon watching Lawrence Welk and that exchange between my parents— my father was the *balance*!

#FinallyLearnedtheLesson

CHAPTER 6

The System

● ● ●

MY FATHER WOULD STAND AT the bottom of the stairs from the main floor and yell in his deep baritone voice, "Marc…Marc…wake up and get dressed so we can get a move on!" When he spoke, we kids would respond. He would always say we needed to "get a move on" or "put some pep in your step." My father thought he was a comedian and would often get a chuckle out of what he was saying, *even* if no one else did. This Saturday morning, he woke me up and prompted me to get dressed so we could take the all-too-familiar ride. Most times, it was just my dad and me out for what was normally a four- to five-hour journey or adventure. We normally took these early on Saturday mornings, and we returned around noon, which gave him plenty of time to finish his sermon for Sunday morning.

Saturday morning was the typical day to sleep in, especially during the months school was in session. I always woke up to cartoons and a bowl of cereal. For an eight-year-old, that's a balanced and nutritional diet! The cereal was put in a cake-mixing bowl, and I always used the large metal spoon that my mother normally used to stir big pots of vegetables. Back in those days, we were not allowed to sit in the living room to watch TV. But, the TV was positioned so that I could sit at the dining room table and watch my normal cartoons: "Shazam," "Fat Albert," "Looney Toons," "The Incredible Hulk," "Superman & Friends," "The Jetsons," and, of course, "The Flintstones." Normally after these went off, I watched "Soul Train," and then it was time to hit the boulevard to hang out with my friends and play some football or just ride our bikes up and down the block.

I got dressed and we jumped into the station wagon. I got to ride in the front seat, which was a rarity; being number six of seven kids, I *never* got to ride shotgun unless I was alone, or it was just my little sister and me in the car. My dad always turned on the radio or put in an eight-track tape, and the car filled with the sounds of gospel music from James Cleveland, Shirley Caesar, or one of his favorites, Mahalia Jackson. We normally made small talk about sports and about what I wanted to be when I grew up. Sometimes the conversations were about school, or we just rode in silence while tapping our feet to the music.

We continued our ride on Highway 80 heading west. It was early in the morning, and I can remember watching the cows as we buzzed by, the 55 mph signs on the highway, and the ride that seemed like forever till we reached our destination. As we pulled in, I saw the huge towers and the twenty-foot barbed wire fences with guards armed with rifles standing watch. It kind of reminded me of when I played with my little green army men, and I would have them standing guard for enemies as they tried to enter my fort; however, this was far from "playland"—this was real life.

We got out of the car and prepared to enter the security area. My dad had what I found out later were "minister credentials," which afforded him certain opportunities to interact with inmates that most never experienced. He was in good standing with the powers that be and still got preferential treatment. We finally entered, got situated, and waited for him to be allowed to come out so that we could begin our visit.

As a kid, I idolized my three older brothers. In my eyes, they were the biggest, baddest dudes to walk the planet, and there was only one man who could beat them at anything—yep, you guessed it—the old man! My parents were significantly older than I was. The year I was born, my father turned forty years old, and my mother turned thirty-eight. By the time I came along, my brothers were sixteen, fourteen, and thirteen; by the time I was of age, many mistook me for their child instead of the younger brother. This particular brother and his wife took me everywhere. I can remember sitting on my brother's lap driving all around Omaha while he worked the pedals.

My brother emerged from a gated area and he was wearing freshly ironed jean pants with a matching jean shirt. He shook my father's hand, and he gave me a hug and said in his famous words, "What's up, boy? You're not still cryin', being a sissy, are you?" We sat and talked, and he told my father how he was going to change and how he would never come back to the "pen," ever. My father explained that he would never visit this facility in the future, and made certain that he knew that he would be on his own if he ever decided to return.

(And he *meant that!*) After our visit, we gathered our belongings from the lockers provided and returned to the car for our long ride home.

I can remember asking my father why he couldn't just leave with us, and why he had to stay there. Why did we have to go through security and have our personal items locked in a locker? Most importantly, *what* did he do to be put in that position? My father explained how the law worked and about responsibility and accountability, but in a manner a child could understand. After several more visits, I began to stop asking the questions on the ride home, but observed everything that happened prior to us departing, during our rides, how the guards interacted with the prisoners, and how my father looked when we left. My brother did more time after that first stint in the Nebraska State Penitentiary. He returned in 1983 until 1989 and again from 1991 to 1995. My father often said that he prayed that I would not be lost or have to go to the penitentiary to learn the lessons of life.

As I look back over all the hills, hurdles, and roadblocks my father and mother had to endure with two of my siblings, I began to see that I didn't want to live caged like an animal or to have my freedom stripped from me. I didn't want to limit potential earnings by tarnishing my reputation with a record. During those years, my father was very transparent; he allowed me to go with him so that I could see for myself where being on the opposite side of the law could land me. He answered all my questions regarding why my brother was there and why he couldn't be released. He explained that the judicial system can be an endless road to nowhere, and many were choosing this route. My father had shown me by being a living example of what a man can become by choosing the path of righteousness, and he allowed me to *see* the example of a man who chooses the path of destruction.

I promised myself long ago that I would *never* be a statistic, that I would never choose the path of destruction, and that I would make every attempt to live life as a reflection of both my parents.

#FinallyLearnedtheLesson

CHAPTER 7

MOMMA

● ● ●

IT WAS A COOL FALL Sunday in 1977 and, just like every other Sunday, we were up and ready for church. This particular Sunday the mass choir sang, and in those days, the choir always marched in from the rear of the church and into the choir stand. I didn't sing this Sunday because I had failed to attend rehearsal the day prior, so I had to sit in the audience and watch with the rest of the congregation.

My mother missed church this Sunday. She had been in and out of the hospital for much of the year. She was in a battle with cancer, and it appeared that she was starting to lose a little ground. After services, my family stopped at McDonald's and ate (my father couldn't boil water). Then my oldest sister, along with my father, went to visit my mother in the hospital. My sixteen-year-old sister was forced to stay at home and babysit my younger sister and me, and we were in my room playing Hot Wheels (yes, one of my favorite things to do—pretend I was really driving).

My door opened slowly, and I can remember looking up and seeing my sister's flushed face, which looked as if it had been overcome with tears. "What's wrong with you?" I asked. She stood silent for a moment, and then let the words flow (I can still hear them clearly, more than thirty-nine years later).

"Momma is dead…"

PAUSE

"Stop lying," I said as I returned to my Hot Wheels.

"I'm not lying!" she responded with more tears in her eyes.

SILENCE

My mother had prepared us for this day for more than two years, as she knew that her days were numbered and wanted to ensure that we would continue to look after one another after she was gone. She would remind me that I was my sister's keeper, and that it was my job to continue to watch out for her as we grew from being children to teenagers and finally adults. She would take my hand and say, "Marc, you have to make sure your sister is OK—make sure you watch out for her." I hated those talks because I didn't want to come to terms with knowing that someday she wouldn't be here. So we all huddled in my room, where my sister allowed us to squeeze her between the two of us. *Life* had forever changed! On October 16, 1977, my mother passed on a cool fall Sunday evening. She was laid to rest on Saturday, October 22, 1977.

The following Sunday, my father got up to preach. He had on a black robe with large "tassels" bearing a cross on the front, hanging from each shoulder. He stood, opened up his Bible, and paused for what seemed to be an eternity. There was *total silence*—enough to hear a pin drop on shag carpet. When he began to speak, he started by thanking the congregation for all the food and support the previous week. He thanked the women of the church for their role in ensuring that the guests were served during the repast. He also thanked the members of the choir who were able to take off work to attend the services, and he thanked the ministers who spoke such kind words.

He then took a *deep* breath and, with eyes closed, began to describe the moment he lost the love of his life. He stated that after she took her last breath, he stayed to take care of some last-minute business. He explained that as he was leaving the hospital, he was sad, yet rejoicing at the same time. As he was walking through the doors of the hospital to leave, "it was like having an anvil removed from my chest." I never witnessed my father cry during that time. I've watched him speak at several funerals that would have made *most* men buckle under the pressure: Richard Glenn Nichols, firstborn (June 1985), Anthony Louis Nichols, second born (March 2004), and Adglee Thompson, mother (2003). I'm sure he had his private moments, but he never shed a tear in public or where we could see. I always knew it was because of his faith and not because he didn't care.

I can hear him saying, "Don't dare waste time shedding tears for me; save those tears for someone who is lost, not saved, and on their way to eternal damnation. I have allowed Christ to order my footsteps, and I know heaven is my home." I learned that death is certain, and it matters *not* how you go, but whether *you* have a relationship with *He* who is able to keep you from falling!

#FinallyLearnedtheLesson

CHAPTER 8

Tough Decisions

● ● ●

MY MOTHER *LOVED* DOGS. As far back as I can remember, we always had a lot of dogs in our home. There was Sheba (a brown German Shepherd—she looked like the dog on the Kalkan label back in those days). We had Diablo (also a German Shepherd, but black in color), Tracy (a black-and-white mutt, small in stature, probably about forty-five pounds—but very smart), and then there was PT, short for Pretty Thang (my mother really liked the way he looked—he was a black-and-white shepherd/husky mix). In our backyard, we had kennels that housed our dogs except Tracy—he was my mother's favorite and, because he was smaller and smarter than the others, she allowed him to live inside the house. I don't know if my father really approved of Tracy living in the house; however, he never voiced his opinion on it if he didn't. During the cold winter months in Omaha, we would routinely allow the dogs to sleep in the basement. Our basement was not a finished living space; the floor was bare concrete and was mainly used to store old unwanted items and some of our games that we rarely used (Ping-Pong and air hockey tables). My mother also did our laundry in the basement, as the washer and dryer were located down there. The other dogs were *not* allowed in the living area of the home often! Every year we would go to the annual church conventions (I can't remember ever missing a convention that normally took place every July). During this time of the year, one of my siblings (normally an older brother) ensured that the dogs were fed and allowed to run free in the yard.

In the early years, most of my brothers and sisters went to Saratoga Elementary School. It was the neighborhood school when my family lived off Twenty-Fifth and Sprague. Because my mother was familiar with Saratoga, she required all of us to attend school there. Even when we moved to a new neighborhood, we continued to attend Saratoga. Most mornings my mother would drop us (my older sister and me) off at school and pick us up at the end of the day; however, when her illness began to take hold, we started to ride the bus. Our home was located on Thirty-Sixth Street, three blocks south of Ames Avenue. Saratoga was located approximately twelve blocks east, down Ames Avenue to Twenty-Fourth and Ames. My sister was in the sixth grade, and I was probably about six years old when we began to catch the city bus to school and back. Each day we would depart our home, take a left, go up the hill, cross over Boyd Street and Taylor Street, and then finally get to Ames, where we would catch the bus to Twenty-Fourth and Ames. Our bus stop was located across the street from Bickles Butcher Shop; I remember the building having a picture of a cow or a statue of a cow, which helped identify it as a butcher shop.

Every morning, our dog Tracy would leave with us, walk us to the bus stop, and return home. Back in those days, there were no cell phones. Once we left the home, we were trained to act accordingly, and we would give the briefing of our day's events upon our return. Tracy returning home alone every day also let my mother know that we had made it safely to the bus stop and were on our way school. My mother often called a good friend of hers, Sister Odessa King, who lived in view of the bus stop (about Twenty-Sixth and Ames, which is now the entrance to Sorenson Parkway going toward Eppley Airfield), who verified that we got on the bus and were heading to school.

Every afternoon, my sister (who was in charge of us departing and arriving safely) and I would return on the bus to Thirty-Sixth Street. If we had money, we would sometimes go into Spoons (neighborhood arcade/candy store) to cop some candy to eat on our way home. And every day, Tracy was waiting for us on the south side of the street in front of North High School and eagerly walked us home. I know this sounds like some Old Yeller or Lacey-type stuff, but it's true—Tracy was one of the smartest dogs I've ever personally come in contact with in my entire life!

As I got older, my sister moved on to junior high school, my younger sister started school, and Tracy was still playing an important part in our lives. He continued to walk us to the bus stops and accompany us when we went to different streets like Taylor, Boyd, or Thirty-Sixth Avenue to play and hang out with friends. After my mother passed, my father began to get rid of the dogs; one by one, they were given away to neighbors or family friends. My father was not in a position to take care of them because of his occupation, and my sisters were getting older, moving off to college and beginning their lives—*all* were gone except Tracy! Tracy had visibly slowed down quite a bit after my mother's death; you could tell that her absence also affected him, and perhaps he wasn't being treated with the same type of love that he had once known from my mother. She would treat him like one of the kids: he slept on the floor on her side of the bed, he often followed her around the house like a toddler would a mother until he was confident of his surroundings, and he was her consummate companion.

One day, after returning from football practice, I took my bike down to the basement and changed clothes (I stored my bike in the basement and also changed out of my football gear down there—my football gear was not allowed in the living area because of the smell). I came into the kitchen from the basement door and, of course, I was ready to eat. However, I was always required to wash prior to entering the kitchen and before eating. I washed, dressed, and came down for dinner. Everyone was home, but there was no Tracy (if everyone was home, he would normally be meandering around the house as well). My father sat us down and explained that Tracy had been sick for some time. He had taken Tracy to the veterinarian. The prognosis was not good, and Tracy was in pain. My father told us that he had to make a decision, and decided that it was best if he put him to sleep so that he would not be forced to suffer any longer.

SILENCE

For me, he had become a part of the family. Anytime I was wandering off into trouble, Tracy was there to warn my mother or to ensure I got home safely. He had walked us to the bus stop for as long as I could remember and would return every evening to make sure we made it home safely. He intervened on my behalf on more than one occasion during altercations that took place at the bus stop. He even attacked the neighborhood bully who lived on Taylor Street when he wanted to beat me up—Tracy had become more than just a pet! That evening I went to my room and cried crocodile tears; he was the *last* reminder of my mother in the house, something we all shared together, and I was feeling the pain from his being put to death (I thought of my father as the executioner)! Years later, I wouldn't allow my children to get a dog; they wanted one and continued to ask for one their entire lives, and I would not give in.

As I write this story I can remember thinking that nothing is forever, and to own a pet is just heartache waiting to happen because eventually the pet will die. I blamed my father for not allowing him to go "naturally" into that dark night and for failing to give us an opportunity for that last good-bye. However, as I have matured and become a man, I have learned that everything must die and nothing is forever. I've learned that we are ALL terminal, pet or not, and that we are all traveling down the same road; eventually we will meet the same fate.

My father taught me that being a man is not only being a man during good times, but also making decisions that will not be popular or accepted by everyone. He taught me that sometimes what appears to be cruel can also be compassionate. He taught me that sometimes we *must* do things that even we don't want to for the good of all. Finally, he taught me that being a man is not a popularity contest. It's a learning process that will never be perfected, but when identified by others, it will eventually be respected!

#FinallyLearnedtheLesson

CHAPTER 9

PK

● ● ●

THE OLD SAYING GOES THAT PKs (preachers' kids) are the worst. I don't know where that saying comes from, but some really believe it to be true. Since I stayed in trouble by doing something stupid or off the wall, I was probably considered the poster child!

In my younger years, my father used to drive a truck for a living (can't remember the name of the company), and he would always bring home a lot of ginger snap cookies. So I think he was driving for a cookie company vendor. I would always ask to ride with him when he was on his route, and occasionally he would allow me to tag along—back then, we were pretty tight. But, there was one place I really hated going with him—and it seemed like I was there every Sunday (Sunday school/church/second service), Wednesday (Bible study), Friday (choir rehearsal), and Saturday (usher/choir rehearsal). It was the main reason I hated going to church—it was my second "unwanted" home. Not only were we the first ones there because he had to open the door, but we were also the last ones to leave *every time!*

The year was 1979, and I was about twelve years old. Well, anyone from the O-NE knows that Saturday night was reserved for Creature Features, *and many late nights we (my three sisters and I) would sit up and scare the bejesus out of one another watching the show.*

Every Sunday morning, my father woke up early enough to make pancakes and woke each one of us up by yelling up the stairs for my three sisters and me to get up and get ready for church. We would eat breakfast, put our clothes on, and head to Sunday school (me cussin' and fussin' all the way!). This Sunday was like any other—after Sunday school, there was a small intermission where we could hang with our friends and chill, talk,

25

cut up, or get into some trouble. Back then, there wasn't a "praise team"—it was called devotion, and it was normally led by a deacon who sometimes didn't know the words, but just hummed along. (The name that comes to mind is Brother Watson.) After he finished murdering whatever hymn it was, he would always address the youth. Please don't ask me what he was saying because I bet there ain't nobody in the Church of the Living God (COTLG) who could tell you what he was saying!

Back in those days, my father always wore a long robe with some type of neat design, and he would enter after devotion and just before the choir sang the last song. One Sunday, I wasn't ushering or singing in the choir. I was just a kid hanging out with whomever, trying to find a comfortable bench to sleep on (yeah, that was nonexistent) or a tic-tac-toe game. (I know what you're thinking, and yep, you're probably right—this sounds like trouble.) My father was looong-winded when it came to sermons. Often babies would cry or little kids would be falling asleep from boredom, and he would often say to the parent, "Let him cry! It's OK; I can talk over them," or "Let her sleep—she can still hear and get the message." Ummmm, well heck, that should be no problem—I should be able to sleep, too, or so I thought.

Well, it was so not the case for me! I had inadvertently fallen asleep while he was preaching, and I can only tell you what my friends described happened next. See, my father had this thing—he would come out of the pulpit and walk around the church and speak (no mic needed), and he could walk and talk (if you were around back then, you know what I'm talking about). Well, he eventually rolled up on me and did a "sleep-by" (that's where I was sleeping in the pew and he rudely awakened me). He grabbed the back of my collar and lifted me off my feet (all while continuing to preach), walked me down to the front of the church, turned and placed me ever so gently into the first pew (yeah, right—it wasn't gentle), and whispered in my ear these words I will never forget: **"Fall asleep up here again if you want to! Ladies and gentlemen, that was a dare—not an invitation!"**

Although I dreaded going to church, it's one of the first places I visit when I return to the home front—so many memories of good people, and I can *always* still find *love* and acceptance. And although I didn't know it then, I know it now—*I finally learned the lesson!*

#AndHeWillNotDepartfromIt

CHAPTER 10

WALK

● ● ●

WINTERS IN THE CITY CAN be harsh and very cold. Many days I can recall having to put on long underwear and dressing in layers before leaving the house in order to stay warm. Even to this day I hate breathing *hot* air; it's stuffy, and it feels as if I can't breathe. On the contrary, I enjoy the summer heat and require an air conditioner and a fan to bring me relief and better breathing. I prefer the air and fan to braving the winter months.

Back in the day, we lived in a two-story home with a basement. My room was located on the second floor above the living room, facing Thirty-Sixth Street. The rooms in those old houses were huge (or maybe it was just that I was little, and they seemed larger than life). On the right wall of my room was a twin bed, and on the left wall were twin bunk beds. I still had enough room to have a racecar track or play with Hot Wheels in the middle of the floor. Behind the left wall was a semi-walk-in closet, and between the two beds were two windows. Because of my breathing issues, my parents allowed me to have a small window air conditioner in my room. I would run that air conditioner all year round, even during the winter months. My sisters, who were cold-natured and loved the heat, would always put a towel under the crack of my door to keep the cold air from entering our small hallway during the winter. My father eventually caught on to my having the air conditioner on during the winter, and removed it from my room. He then instructed me to open the window. He said the air outside is colder than the machine could produce—*and it's free*!

It was a cold winter Sunday morning, and the family was up as usual and preparing to depart for Sunday school and church services. We all piled into the station wagon and began our journey. We were driving to church, and it was super-de-duper cold outside. I was in the backseat, whining about the high temperature, pulling at my collar, fidgeting, and just being all-around irritable. The church was approximately seven to eight miles from our home, and it would normally take no more than ten minutes' driving time. But due to the ice and snow, my father was taking it easy, and it would be no more than fifteen minutes until we arrived.

I yelled to my father for the fifth or sixth time, "It's *hot* in here—can you turn down the heat? Dang!" The church is on Twentieth and Binney, and we had just rounded the corner across from Howard Kennedy Elementary School on Thirtieth and Binney—a full ten blocks from the church. My father had had enough, pulled the car over, and said, *"Get out."*

I replied, "Huh?"

He never said another word—he looked at me with *"the look"* that told me he had had enough, and the best thing for me to do was get out of the car. I got out of the car, and he pulled off away from the curb and headed toward the church. He never looked back, and I began my ten-block journey in what I thought was probably single-digit weather. I can remember the wind ripping through my flimsy pant legs. My shoes were hard on the bottom and didn't bend at the toe, which made it even harder to walk on the ice. My hands were cold (I wasn't wearing gloves because I was in the car), and I can remember thinking it was a good thing I had a hat and a coat with a hood or I would really be cold. I finally made it to the church, where I went to the restroom and begin running hot water on my hands in an attempt to bring the feeling back.

I know most are going to say how cruel, cold, or borderline abusive that must have been. Looking back, I finally think I understand. You can rest assured that I didn't complain about the heat anymore or how I couldn't breathe. I would always remember that day, and before I started whining, I would remember that he didn't have a problem using the old expression, "pat and turners"—pat them feet and turn them corners!

One thing a *man* cannot be is a whiner. He will experience uncomfortable situations that he will not like; he may be required to perform a job or tasks that he may not prefer; yet, he *must* endure uncomfortable situations, and it is unacceptable for him to cry or whine like an infant. He must be willing to make sacrifices, no matter the size.

Finally, a *"man"* learns from a man (whether it be neighbors, coaches, pastors, teachers, counselors, or his own *dad*) how to be a *man*!

#FinallyLearnedtheLesson

CHAPTER 11

Dating

● ● ●

IT HAD BEEN A FEW months since my mother had passed, and we were finally adjusting to life after her death. In the beginning, many of the parishioners (mostly women) brought food over almost daily so that we (kids) didn't starve. You see, back in those days, my father had no clue how to cook, clean, or wash and fold clothes. Eventually the food stopped coming, and we were left to fend for ourselves. On Sundays, we always had McDonald's, A&W, or Kentucky Fried Chicken (KFC) for dinner. My father began to muddle around the kitchen, and soon he was actually making stuff that was edible (who knew). Although we would still be invited out for dinners or over to people's homes, we were starting to function as a small family again. With my mother gone, my father began to assume both roles in the house. With the four of us helping (my three sisters and me), we slowly started the healing process, and life began to go back to normal. My mother would *always* be a missing piece of the puzzle. But she had filled us with her love and knowledge so that we could continue to push ahead.

I loved the "after church" activities that we had on Youth Sunday. On those Sundays, before the sermon was finished, my nostrils took in the sweet aroma from the ovens in the kitchen—cinnamon rolls, Rice Crispy Treats, hot dogs, and much more. The same women made these treats once a month, and the proceeds from the "bake sale" went back to the youth organization my mother once chaired, the YPPU (Young People Progressive Union). This was one of the few times my father shelled out money, and we could buy just about anything we wanted. Now the same women had made the same treats for as long as I can remember. But, if one of them made something different, it was gonna be a problem because kids and adults alike could never get enough of the great treats they brought. One of the women who made hot dogs was always very friendly to my sister and me. She would give us free hot dogs and was *always* more than kind.

One day my father told my sister and me that we were going out to eat. He wanted us home early so that we could dress and get a move on.

Back in those days, after my mother had passed, my younger sister and I mainly played on the block with our friends. My father didn't make a lot of money, so he had to use money wisely and make it stretch until the next payday. I remember him saying once that he made $300 a week as the pastor of the church, and he always worked a few other jobs to help make ends meet...

So my sister and I got dressed, my father came home and bathed, and we all jumped in the car (me shotgun, of course) and headed out to eat. This was a very rare occasion to be going out for dinner on a weekday. I was a very observant kid—I listened to everything. I would hide under my sister's bed, unbeknownst to my sister, and listen to her and her friends talk about anything and everything. I would also eavesdrop on my parents when they had discussions, and mainly paid attention to anywhere I had gone in a car—I could tell you how to get to wherever and back with no problem. When relatives would come in from out of town, my mother would tell me to get in the car with them and take them wherever it was that they needed to go. I can remember one couple asking, "You sure he knows how to get us there and back?" and she said, yes, he knows. I could take them to any family member's home and return without missing a turn.

We were in the car, and we headed down Thirty-Sixth Street, took a left on Paxton Boulevard until we got to Bedford, took a left to Thirtieth Street, and then made a quick right. We rode all the way down Thirtieth Street, passing the Stage II Lounge on the right, New Hope Baptist Church on the left, and Maxi Walker on the right near Hamilton Street. We crossed over Cuming Street with Roberts Dairy on the left and Tech High School on the right, and then came to the street that divided the city from north to south, Dodge Street. We took a right on Dodge and then, in less than two hundred yards, made a right into an apartment complex. Back in 1978, that building housed multiple apartments. Some years later, I believe it became a nursing home, and it is now a commercial property.

You can imagine my dismay that we had turned into an apartment complex. We were told we were going *out* to dinner, not to someone's home. We exited the car and took the elevator to the fourth floor (I think), and to our surprise, guess who opened the door—a woman we had known our entire lives! She was always very nice to us and gave us hot dogs during those YPPU bake sales once a month at the church—Sister F is what I will call her. She was just as nice in her home as she was at church every Sunday, and she really took a liking to my sister and me. She catered to our every need, and started to fill a void that was left with the passing of my mother.

As young kids, my sister and I were *very* impressionable—we didn't have a clue about dating, men liking women, women liking men, courting, or any of the other dynamics in a relationship. Sister F began to take us shopping at Target, JCPenney—heck; we were even going to stores in Council Bluffs, Iowa, that cost a lot of money. She began to help pay for my extracurricular activities such as track and basketball. For my eleventh birthday, she even bought me a yellow Schwinn dirt bike with the heavy-duty spokes in the tires; it was the talk of the neighborhood, and everyone wanted one. The bike cost Sister F about $300. Shoot, back in 1978, that was a mint! That bike was stolen from me about a week later when one of the neighborhood girls took off on it without my permission while I was playing football on the boulevard. She and some other girls took it to Safeway on Thirty-Second and Ames, and someone took it from her.

Things were going well. My sister and I had a "mother" figure, and she gave us all the attention we could ever want. However, something or someone always comes into the picture to cast aspersions or doubt with regard to a newly developed relationship, and my sister and I were used as pawns in the game. The whispers began in the home, as well as in the church, about the relationship that was developing between my father and Sister F, and those rumors began to affect the bond that had been developing with our new mother figure and us. We began to look at Sister F as though she had been planning to get her hooks into my father even before my mother died—she was only nice to us because she wanted to be close to my father, and she really didn't care about us—she only wanted to be the coveted first lady of the Church of the Living God. And, my friends, once you allow the devil to enter into the details, it is the beginning of the end of *any* relationship!

My sister and I began to give Sister F a hard time. We didn't want to spend time with her, and we didn't want any gifts, shopping sprees, mother figure time, hot dogs—anything she had to offer. My father was forced to move on, explore other opportunities, and date other women. I am positive she was hurt in the process, but she could no longer endure disobedient children. I often look back at those days and regret that my sister and I allowed "others" to mislead us to believe the "whispers" by those in the congregation and those who lived under our own roof.

My father believed in the sanctity of marriage, and he believed that man was not meant to live alone. He also believed that his children needed a mother in the home who could help raise them and provide a mother's perspective. What we didn't realize or know was that my father was going to marry someone whether we liked it or her or not. We may have ruined that one relationship, but he had learned a lesson, and it would be different next time.

I learned that some people will never accept change, and that some people will manipulate a situation to get the outcome they want. I also learned that sometimes the grass is not greener on the other side. Finally, I learned that a few bad intentions or actions can change the course of someone's life forever. I spoke with Sister F some years later, and I didn't get to apologize as I had wanted. You could see in her eyes that she *loved* my sister and me—yes, even before my mother passed—and she never treated us any differently. We exchanged pleasantries, but I just didn't know how to say I was sorry for the pain I caused in her life.

However, I have gone to the mirror and apologized to myself for my role in breaking up my father's relationship with a woman who had known us from birth and probably loved us as if we were her own. My actions directly affected *my* life, causing me to go down the road less traveled, and causing a strain in my relationship with my father. I recognized that I was my own worst enemy, and my actions would haunt me until I became a man.

#FinallyLearnedtheLesson

CHAPTER 12

Be There

● ● ●

MY FATHER WAS A NO-NONSENSE kind of guy. He believed in family, and made no bones about us being in a scuffle or a "fisticuffs," as he would call it—as long as it wasn't with those in the family! Years ago, everyone in our neighborhood was bused to school; integration was hot and heavy on the political agenda, and we were the pawns in the integration game. As fate would have it, we were bused to Lincoln Elementary in South Omaha (it was located not far from the downtown Omaha post office), and every morning we would get up and walk to the bus stop on Paxton Boulevard and Thirty-Sixth Street. I liked to pick on my little sister (she was an easy target) just like any other brother or sister (as I was also my older sisters' favorite target), and we would fight like cats and dogs. My father didn't believe in hitting women, and he was adamant about me not touching my sister as well. Anytime she ran and told on me, I received more than a few knots upside my head or ended up with a raw rear. That was just the way it was; we fought, she lost and told, and I received the butt kicking of the week.

My sister had gotten into a "scuffle" at school and, just like any normal kid, she told my dad. He asked all the questions regarding the fight, and talked to her about trying to talk her way out of it. It ended up that someone was bullying my sister. It just so happened that he was a boy from the neighborhood, and he attended our church (part-time). At that time, I was in the sixth grade and she was in the fourth. The talk lasted awhile, and I was just there listening. I, on the other hand, needed *no* encouragement to defend myself—I fought on a regular basis and wouldn't hesitate to get into a "scuffle" or two! My father turned to me and asked where I was during her fight. I told him that I wasn't there and didn't even know that she had been in a fight. ***LONG PAUSE*** My father looked at me with a straight face, never cracked a smile, and said, "Next time, you better *be there!*" Now for those of you who are slow, that meant that if she came home one more time and told him that she was fighting a boy, there would be a misunderstanding and I would bear the brunt for the lack of communication. I received the message, and it was *crystal clear*! I knew my father meant business. He wasn't playing when it came to her being picked on or bullied, and as quiet as it was kept, I wasn't very happy that I had to be put in check for something I didn't even do. So this kid was in big trouble—and he didn't even know it!

Lincoln Elementary looked more like an apartment building (which it eventually became) than a school. It was a brick building, three stories high, with a ten-foot fence around the perimeter. Unlike any of the schools in North Omaha, Lincoln was very small and had a limited playground area. When facing the school, there was a playground on the left side. We played kickball there or hung out, and it was all cement (much like a school in the middle of New York City). On the right side, it had the standard monkey bars, a sandpit, and a small grass area. It was much like being in a prison. The staircase was huge, and if I recall correctly, the floors looked as if they were made of marble.

A few days later we are at school—and I cannot remember if school was out or if we were just going to lunch—but I was coming down the stairs from the third floor to the main level. The hallway and stairs were packed with kids moving around like roaches when the lights come on (don't act like you don't know about that). As I rounded the final turn on the stairs, I saw my little sister talking to a boy, and she was yelling in his face. Before I could yell out her name, the boy reared back and slapped what looked like the taste out of her mouth. That slap hurt me, and I knew what I had to do to this kid. (*Back in those days, I played the trumpet. I can remember telling my dad I wanted to be in the band at school, and we went out to about Seventy-Fourth and Dodge Street to a music store (it was across the street from the Crossroads at almost the exact spot as Men's Warehouse is today) and rented a trumpet for me to use. I played that trumpet from fourth to seventh grade. I eventually gave it up to play football some years later.*)

As I was coming down the stairs, I had a trumpet case in my hand. The boy who I had just witnessed hit my sister was in the same grade as she, but he was bigger than me. So I knew that I had to handle him like he was an older kid. As I ran down the stairs, the boy saw me, turned toward me, and opened his mouth to say something—but all he received was the trumpet case on the left side of his head! When he staggered back, I was all over him like the janitor—mopping the floors clean! My sister regains her composure and starts kicking the kid. After two or three teachers break up the fight, all three of us end up in the principal's office. Mr. Brooks (I think was his name) was a hip white guy who knew all the slang and could talk the talk. Unfortunately for me, he knew my dad because he was once a teacher at Saratoga (my former school) and, of course, he knew he was a no-nonsense type of parent who didn't tolerate any shenanigans.

Our parents are called, and my dad arrives first. Mr. Brooks explains what went down, and I was able to explain my side along with my sister's side of the story. The one thing Mr. Brooks was unaware of was that although my father was a minister/pastor, that he gave me the marching orders prior to this event even happening; so I already knew as I sat in the office that if she told her story and I told mine, there would be no beat downs later that evening. My father told Mr. Brooks that he understood that we had to be suspended (all three of us were suspended: him for the slap, her for the kick, and me for mopping the floor), but he would not tolerate or allow a boy to hit my sister nor punish me for obeying his orders to *be there*! We left school that day, jumped in the station wagon, and were treated to McDonald's; I had followed my father's order to the letter of the "house law," and now it was time for the reward.

That day I learned that it was OK for me to pick on my sister (so I thought), but no one else was allowed a pass. I also learned that the unwritten code in any home was not to allow *anyone* to violate or beat up your siblings without that person knowing that if he or she wants to fight, pick on, or talk about a family member, he or she will have to contend with all of us. I learned an even more valuable lesson that my mother tried to teach me before she passed: I am my sister's keeper, and my job as an older brother is to make certain that she is safe from all hurt, harm, and danger. This mentality has continued even until today with the females who mean a lot to me.

#FinallyLearnedtheLesson

CHAPTER 13

Fisticuffs

● ● ●

BACK IN THE DAY, I was an average, red-blooded, All-American boy: I loved to play sports, ride bikes, play neighborhood games, run, jump, and tease girls; that's what we did as mischievous youths.

The year was about 1979: I was twelve years old, rambunctious, and *very* angry. After the passing of my mother, I used her death as an excuse to get into physical altercations at school and in the neighborhood. I was in the sixth grade at Lincoln Elementary School located in South Omaha; it was the beginning of the busing era, and we rode the bus thirty to thirty-five minutes to school each way every morning and evening. We shared a bus with other kids who went to Train Elementary School; those kids lived in a neighborhood about five miles from mine.

After school one evening on the bus ride home, one of the kids from Train and I got into fisticuffs on the bus. The fight started on the bus and, in true fight fashion, we fought in the aisles, on the seats, and eventually opening the rear door and finishing in front of Saratoga Elementary School. Saratoga was the central bus stop for the kids from Train. The kid I had the fight with ended up with two black eyes. When his mother found out, she called my father and, of course, I suffered the consequences. In another incident at school, I fought a kid on the playground after he called my mother a name, and I was eventually suspended from school. Fighting had become a pattern for me; if someone said something about my mother, it was as if there was a green light for a knock-down, drag-out fight and it was gonna be a hard-fought battle. When angered, I could feel the rage swell up in me and overheat before fighting.

Each of my siblings who lived in the home had to take turns cleaning the kitchen, which consisted of: washing dishes, cleaning countertops and the dining room table and sweeping the floor. The evening in question, my sister had "cleaning duty." I was out late playing on the boulevard and returned home to eat before calling it a night. In typical sibling fashion my sister, who was in the process of cleaning the kitchen, stopped me from entering the kitchen citing that the kitchen was closed. My sister was older than me and was used to telling me what to do without any pushback; yet, I was growing and starting to develop muscles, and playing football and wrestling helped me with my agility and strength. Our kitchen was small: it was only big enough for maybe three people to fit comfortably and, with some of the extras—kitchen table and dishwasher—there was only room for one more person. The dishwasher was a portable washer that you had to roll into the kitchen and hook up to the sink and run another hose into the sink for the discharge of water after the wash/rinse cycle.

So my sister stops me at the entrance of the kitchen and says, "The kitchen is closed—see you tomorrow." I tell her to stop playing because I'm hungry and wanted to eat. She tells me that I was too late and that I can get something to eat later. My sister is standing on one side of the portable dishwasher (which is situated in the middle of the floor) and I on the other. She is using the dishwasher to keep me from the refrigerator by holding it firmly in place so I can't get around. I can feel my temperature rising, and I suddenly leap over the dishwasher as if she was a running back and I was a middle linebacker—and the fight was on! I guess my father heard the commotion and he is on me in a flash, pulling me off my sister with one hand. As he is putting me down behind him I can hear him yelling at my sister, "I done told you about messin' with this boy!" I had finally gotten the best of my sister, who had tortured me in everything from singing songs about me, beating me at running and, of course, each fight we'd ever had before that day! I was shocked and surprised that I had finally gotten the best of her—*and it felt good*. But it came with a price.

The following Saturday, after our normal church activities, my father took a different route from church. We drove north down Twenty-Fourth Street to Ames Avenue, took a left until we got to the old Safeway, took a quick right on Thirty-First Street, and made another left on Fowler. Now I played ball with some of the homies back in the day in this neighborhood, so I knew the hood well and all the kids who lived in the area. We didn't have gangs back then; we had neighborhood football and basketball teams, and we went from hood to hood playing ball. We rode right by the lot next to the post office, where we played football against this neighborhood. We stopped at an all-too familiar house, and my father got out of the car and told me to get out as well. I'm thinking, *"What are we doing here?"* and *"How does he know about this place?"* We walked up to the door, my father rang the bell, and a woman answered the door. I had never been inside this house; I had only been on the block, hanging out with my friends before and after they went in for practice.

My father asked for Mr. Washington, and we were instructed to go the side of the house through a side entrance into the basement of the home. I will never forget the day I stepped foot into that house. We walked into the house, and Mr. Washington greeted us. I knew this house because several of my friends who boxed came here for practice; it was the home of their coach and trainer, Mr. Carl Washington, or better known as the C.W. Boxing Club. As we entered the basement, you could smell the thick, musty odor. It smelled like the musty gear of three football teams had been lying around for years. On reaching the basement, there were speed bags and heavy bags that hung from the ceiling, an open area for exercise and shadow boxing, and then there was the ring—YES, a boxing ring built right in the middle of this man's basement. Many of the kids who lived in the neighborhood were there practicing and greeted me with the head nod as they continued to work out.

In Omaha, if you wanted to box, you went to the C.W. Boxing Club, and if you wanted to wrestle, you went to Lil Joe; I had no clue my father knew who either of these guys was. My father talked to Mr. Washington about my fighting, and told him that since I enjoyed fighting he wanted me to do it the right way—*in the ring*. I was instructed to be back there Monday afternoon when I would start my new boxing career. I was not excited; I didn't mind fighting, but I didn't want to do it in an organized fashion.

For the next several months, I had worked in that gym day in and day out, training for boxing matches that would eventually come when I was ready. *****NOT SO SURE ABOUT FIGHTING***** After about five months of training, I was finally going to get my chance to fight. We were instructed to pack a small cooler filled with fruits, sandwiches, and drinks; the first team match would take place in Fremont, Nebraska. Two vans were rented for the trip, and we kids piled into the vans early in the morning for the trip out of the hood and out to the "country." I watched a few fights, and then it was *my* turn. I was matched with a kid my age from Fremont. I was in one corner, and he was in the other. We were introduced to the crowd, and of course, the Omaha kids were the visitors, and we were without our parents or family support. Naturally, the spectators were in favor of the hometown kids. **DING**! The bell rang, and we met in the middle of the ring. I remember everything I was taught in practice. We jabbed and moved around the ring. The other fighter was visibly nervous, as was I. So we threw a few more jabs and finally engaged one another. I could feel myself getting the better of him. He was covering his face, and I was hitting him with body blows and a few left and right hooks. He threw some punches but didn't land any, and my confidence began to grow. **DING**! End of the first round! I went to my corner, and the coach told me I was doing good.

DING! The bell rang again and we met in the middle of the ring. There was only one issue—I didn't realize how tired you get from really boxing. I was plumb tuckered out, and the once-scared kid wasn't so scared anymore. He came out punching fast, hard, and frequently—he had me back on my heels guarding my head while he unloaded a barrage of shots to the body. **DING**! He won the round, and I was ready to quit; however, the neighborhood kids were there watching, and I knew I wouldn't live that down when we got back to the hood. **DING**! The bell rang, signaling the final round, and we met in the center of the ring again. I forgot everything I learned and began to swing wildly. The other kid began to swing wildly as well, and we went toe-to-toe in the middle of that ring for what seemed like an eternity. **DING**! The match was over, and we returned to our corners. The match was determined a draw, both our hands were raised, and we each received a small medal for our efforts. The kids in the neighborhood were supportive, and we joked about the fight and I could go home without having to duck my head in shame. That was my first and last fight; when we returned that Saturday evening and I went home, I told my father that I didn't like fighting and that I wouldn't be going back to C.W. Boxing Club.

As I look back over that period of life, I now understand why my father took me over to C.W. Boxing Club. He wanted to let me know that anyone could fight. But, if you wanted to be a real disciplined fighter you had to dedicate yourself to the craft, be conditioned, and be willing to be hit in front of a larger audience than just your friends. I learned that as a parent you can give your kids exactly what they want and allow them to make decisions based on real-life experience. My father taught me a valuable lesson—he encouraged me to fight, but in an acceptable manner, and he allowed me to see the error of my own ways. After that experience, my fights decreased drastically. I knew that my father was serious when he said he would rather I fight in the ring than in the streets, and *if* I didn't want to fight in the ring, I might need to stop fighting in the street. I got a quick lesson in conflict resolution and learned that perhaps everything wasn't worth fighting over.

#FinallyLearnedtheLesson

CHAPTER 14

Ringworm

● ● ●

WE HAD A BIG YARD—THE largest yard on our block and, I believe, in our neighborhood. I believe our neighbor's house caught fire and was eventually demolished. My father then made a great move by buying the land that the other house was on, doubling the size of our property. My father erected a fence to enclose both properties and made it one large yard. I would guesstimate that we had about three-quarters of an acre of land, with a swing set in the back yard; the side yard was just a big field. Thinking back on it, it was a bear to cut that grass, and it took a full morning to complete. The kids in the neighborhood would gather at our house to play games because we had a big yard, and we would play freeze tag, hide-and-seek, kickball, football, and even Simon says. Back in those days, the yard gave us a safe place to play without worrying about running in the streets or any of the other issues that come along with playing outside in the city.

One morning, I woke up during the summer, and I had a rash on the back of my leg. I showed my dad, and we decided to put some over-the-counter ointment on my leg. After a few days of monitoring the rash, it had grown and was itching out of control. My father, like *many* men, hated to go to the doctor, not only because he didn't wanna be seen, but it cost money—money we never really had. We were barely making it, and I imagine my father was still paying hospital bills for my mother's illness prior to her passing. So we ended up going to see Dr. Pressure (he was our family doctor). He was located at about Fifty-First and Ames on the right-hand side if traveling from the north side out west toward Seventy-Second. The doctor diagnosed me with ringworm, and I was provided a prescription, with instructions that I may still be at the contagious stage and should stay out of contact with others for a specific amount of time. My father explained that I couldn't go outside for a few days and should stay away from the other kids and my sisters in the house so that it didn't spread. I almost understood, but I hated that I couldn't go outside because it was a nice warm summer evening and all the kids started to come out to play *in our yard*!

It was a Wednesday evening, and my father gave final instructions to my older sister and me prior to heading off to Bible study. My father pulled off, and I waited until he disappeared down Thirty-Sixth Street, took a left onto the boulevard, and was no longer in sight. Well, like any all-American boy, I was *out* and into the yard to play with the fellas. My sister was sitting on the porch and said, "Daddy said for you to stay in the house." I ignored her and kept moving. I joined in the fun, and the kid on the sideline was able to play with two more players. The two teams met in the middle, and we decided who got the ball first. My team was facing away from the street, and we were set to receive. (Now a few weeks earlier, there was an issue with a small portion of the fence, and it was in the process of being fixed. There was a single pole in the ground but not cemented in, and the fence still needed to be run to the next pole.)

The ball was thrown down to the other end (simulating the kickoff), and guess who caught it and was prepared to take the ball and run it all the way back. Yup, you guessed it—yours truly. I was running the ball, juking and dippin', dodging, and cutting from left to right and right to left, when it seemed like all the other kids kinda just stopped in their tracks. I just figured that they had given up because I was fast, and only one kid posed a problem; we never played on the same team until we were old enough to go down to the boulevard.

Now that I am a parent, I understand parent stuff and how we do what we do, when we do what we do (you follow me?), LOL!

You see, my old man was no dummy. I guess having three boys prior to me and a couple of girls, he knew that the chances of my staying in the house were slim to none. So I imagine that sixth sense kicked in and, just to make sure, he doubled back to check. I turned around after the score and low and behold, my father was working his way down the field behind me. And he wasn't alone— he had pulled up the pole that had not been cemented in yet and was loose in the ground. I was in big trouble, and I knew it. The other kids were frozen;

they weren't moving, and *not* one said a word to warn me that he was coming behind me with bad intentions—some friends they were! So I made a beeline to the house. I ran up to the sidewalk beside the house, past the water hose holder, around to the front of the house, up the stairs, past my sister (who at this point was laughing *very* hard), into the house, up the stairs, and into my room. Somewhere in the cloud of smoke, I lost my father and, by the time I realized that he wasn't on my heels, I was in my room waiting for the inevitable—but it never came. I guess he was late for church and decided against exacting punishment and returned to his car. I had certainly dodged a bullet that day. I am so glad that church was due to start and he didn't have time to put it on me.

I didn't learn very much that day; I would continue to get into trouble for a good portion of my childhood, but I certainly learned how to handle my own children when I became a father. He had prepared me to follow my instincts when I felt that trouble was brewing or the hair on the back of my neck stood up. I often think of these experiences and smile, and I often wish that I could rewind time and do it all over again.

#FinallyLearnedtheLesson

CHAPTER 15

Curfew

● ● ●

I WAS WALKING MY BIKE up Thirty-Sixth Street; the streetlights were already on, and I am thinking to myself that I hope he buys the story that I had concocted and maybe I wouldn't get punishment or a whooping for being late! It had started out a normal Saturday morning with breakfast, cartoons, and Soul Train, and then time to hit the streets and do whatever it was we were going to do in the neighborhood. Most times you could find the kids at Druid Hill (the local elementary school) playing basketball, on the boulevard playing tackle football, or even at Fontenelle Park playing football or basketball or feeding the ducks. Back in the day, there was never a dull moment in the hood, and we made certain to find the happening spots and play until it was time to go home. I was twelve years old, and the rules for EVERY kid in the neighborhood was the same: in before the streetlights came on and, if you missed it, there was gonna be some consequences and repercussions! Now *everyone* knew this—so there was no excuse for anyone to come home late.

This day I decided to roll down to my aunt's house on Eighteenth and Wirt Street. Her house was located around the corner from my father's church, which was maybe seven or eight miles away—so it wasn't a short bicycle ride. My aunt had a basketball court built behind her home. She did this so she could keep an eye out for the neighborhood kids and provide them with a safe haven in her yard. She was the neighborhood grandmother; *everyone* knew that if you came to "Grammy G's" house, you must be on your best behavior because she didn't allow shenanigans in her yard. The same neighborhood kids also played football directly across the street from her home in an empty field (which is now a park, I believe, dedicated to state senator Ernie Chambers).

After playing basketball and football, my two cousins, some of the other neighborhood kids, and I were allowed to go in the house and play Intellivision. (This was the premier gaming system of the era that very few had; it was expensive and had great graphics.) My cousins and I would take turns playing hockey, baseball, football, and basketball. We were *very* competitive and would cheat to win! It started getting late, and my aunt informed me that it might be time for me to go. She even offered to take me home, but that would mean leaving my bike at her house—and who knows when I would get it again. Back in those days, your bike was your mode of transportation; we rode those things all over the north side of Omaha and without one, you either had to ride doubles or run behind your friends. ****Not an Option****

I started my trip to the house a lot later than anticipated. Because my aunt's home was out of the range of where I was supposed to be, I would normally say that I was elsewhere if asked. As I was riding, I finally made it to Thirtieth and Wirt (before the North Freeway was built, you could take these streets all the way to Thirtieth), took a right, and rode down toward the famous Timeout Chicken spot. I noticed it was starting to get dark fast, and I could see the lights flickering as they warmed up. *All* kids in the hood know when they hear the humming sound from the street lights that it's time to make a move toward your home so that when your parents look outside, at a minimum you're in the yard, and you save yourself from punishment. I continued on my journey around Druid Hill and onto the boulevard. By the time I reached Thirty-Fourth Street, the lights are full on and it was dark outside. When I reached the bottom of my street, I had to think of something to tell the old man so that I wouldn't be in too much trouble.

THE PLAN I devised a plan: I would stop at the bottom of my street and let the air out of my front tire, and I was thinking, "*This should work if I walk my bike up the hill and say that I caught a flat on the way home, and that's why I am late.*" Yeah, yeah—that should work! I reached the house, opened the front gate, walked my bike up the front walk, and carried it onto the porch. We had a large front porch like the Victorian homes you see in the Deep South. We would put chairs out, sit, and watch traffic. Some people enclosed their porches and used them as sunrooms. My father, in true fashion, opened the front door and emerged from the shadows. "Son, where ya been—you're late." I explained that I was at Druid Hill playing basketball, and I had a flat tire. I had to walk my bike home, and that's why I didn't make curfew. ***SILENCE***

My father turned, walked into the house, and left me standing on the porch. **SIGH OF RELIEF** I normally kept my bike in the basement, as I was not allowed to bring it through the house, so I began to go back down the stairs to take my bike through the back door. My father called out my name, "Marc." It was as if I was at a party and the DJ scratched the record. I turned to see my father holding an orange object in his hand. Upon closer review, I could see it was the air pump. "Bring the bike back up here and let's see what the problem is." My father had this li'l smirk that told me *everything* I needed to know: I was found out, and it wasn't going to be pretty! After using the pump, my father sat long enough to realize that the tire was not going to deflate and stared at me for what seemed to be an eternity! My father had beaten me at my own game; he called my bluff, and now I was probably going to get exactly what was coming to me. My father had me put my bike away, and he allowed me time to marinate before coming to handle business later that evening.

My father showed me that night that even though I thought I was slicker than a can of oil, he had already mastered the game of deceit and deception. Chances were that anything I could think of to try to outfox him, he had already experienced with my five older siblings. I learned that I would have to get up pretty early in the morning to pull the wool over my father's eyes, and even then, it more than likely wouldn't work. I also learned that it was much easier to go with the program and abide by the rules; I was just making it harder for myself if I continued to go against the grain.

#FinallyLearnedtheLesson

CHAPTER 16

On the Run

• • •

"HE SAID IT'S OK IF you come over"—that's how it started! Back in the day, we didn't have cell phones, pagers, Facebook, Twitter, Myspace or FaceTime—we only had landlines, notes in school, and you either went to someone's house or met up on the block (a hangout place in the neighborhood).

The house at 4210 North Thirty-Sixth Street, Omaha, Nebraska, was the only home and hood I knew—I had never lived anywhere else. It was a great place to grow up. Almost every Saturday morning and on most holidays, you could find all the neighborhood kids gathered on Paxton Boulevard, playing football. People would sometimes park on the side street to watch us play—especially those older dudes who used to play in the neighborhood, until adulthood caught up to them. At this time, the local high school, North High, decided to expand. Their great plan was to buy a portion of the homes in the neighborhood, which sent the homeowners packing. We moved to the new neighborhood the summer of my thirteenth birthday. Moving was a sad occasion; it was like leaving behind everything and everyone you knew. We moved to what I would call a nice neighborhood where the houses were a little more modern and had bigger yards. The kids in the neighborhood were mostly nice and accepting, but it wasn't the same—I knew it was going to take some getting used to. One thing that made *everything* better about any move for a thirteen-year-old boy is *girls*. This neighborhood had a plethora of girls, and most of them lived on one street—Camden Avenue.

"*She*" had caramel skin, long flowing hair, and a body that could drive a thirteen-year-old to do some things that would change his life. *She* was one of the first girls I ever looked at differently than just a playmate or a friend.

During the summer months in Omaha, all the kids in the city went to Creighton University's summer youth program (designed to give the kids in the city something to do, with a variety of activities). All of the neighborhood kids would gather at the designated bus stop to attend Creighton. This was my opportunity to get to know the kids in the neighborhood—especially *her!* One day while on the phone, *she* told me that it was OK for me to come over and visit with her; her dad said it was OK. Her father was known in the neighborhood as a no-nonsense kind of guy, which means he didn't take too kindly to the neighborhood boys talking to his beautiful young daughter. Although I found it hard to believe that he gave permission for her to have company, I was a thirteen-year-old boy with raging hormones and willing to walk in the middle of a fire with gasoline underwear on to get close to *her!*

In this neighborhood, many of the houses were built as split-level homes: when you walk in the front door, you have the option to either go downstairs to the basement or go upstairs into the living room. As we sat in her living room talking and laughing, she suddenly looked up and yelled, ***PAUSE***...*The living room faces the front of the home and sits up high: from there you can see the driveway and each car that rides in front of the home. Behind the couch is the kitchen, equipped with a sliding glass door that leads to the deck. The deck is about a story off the ground with stairs attached, and this could be used as an entrance to the home or as a great area to sunbathe or grill...*

"*He's home*—you have to go!"

I looked out the big glass window and saw a gray Seville pulling into the driveway. I said, "But you said he said I could come over."

She yelled, "*I lied!*" ***OH @#^%!***

Now back in the day, I was a normal kid. I played football, boxed, wrestled, swam, ran track, and played basketball—I had no problems running and jumping and gettin' somewhere fast! So I bolted—jumping over the couch, running through the kitchen, and opening the sliding glass door. Forgoing the stairs, I jumped over the side of the deck. I looked back and he was coming around the side of the house. Now he's probably about forty-plus and, well, I'm thirteen with some pretty good wheels, so he wasn't gaining ground, let alone catching me. I ran across an open field to Fort Street and into the woods (I believe these are homes for seniors now). I worked my way through the woods up to Hartman and then bobbed and weaved my way to my house. With my heart beating fast, I came in the house and went straight to the basement, where I sat on my bed, wondering if he was still out there searching for me.

A few weeks earlier, on a Saturday afternoon, my father told me to cut the grass. Now instead of doing as I was told, I deliberately disobeyed his orders. With the next day being Sunday, I really should have done what I was told to do since that was the night to go to Skateland—everyone who is anyone went skating on Sunday nights in Omaha. *She* told me she was going skating this Sunday and asked if I was going, and my reply was, "If you're going, I'm going." After church dinner, I asked my father if I could go skating, and his answer was, "Yes, as soon as the grass is cut." Now it was dang-near dark outside—too late to cut grass—and he wasn't budging on his answer; so I did what any thirteen-year-old boy with raging hormones would do—*I went skating!*

When I returned from skating, I figured I would do my usual: go into the car and open the garage door just a bit, roll under the door, and enter the house via the garage entrance—yeah—he took the garage door opener out of the car. Plan B: knock on my older sister's window and ask her to open the door—but she looked out the window and shook her head no. "Daddy is upstairs waiting for you," she said. ****@^%)**** I went to my younger sister's room, and the same thing happened. My father had already told them not to assist me in my attempts to sneak in and that he would be waiting for me in the living room. So I was forced to knock on the door, and my father answered. I walked in, and he stopped me cold in my tracks. "So you think you're grown, huh?"

"No."

"So you just gonna leave when I told you that you had to cut that grass first, huh?"

PAUSE

"Yes."

The next thing I knew, my father had taken his fist and swung it from Mississippi, hitting me in my chest. I could feel my chest grab his fist and hold on! I hit the wall and slid down to my knees, and he began to speak to me. "Oh, so you're a man now? Get up, *get up!*" I stood up and caught another one. He told me to get to my room and not to leave the house until he said I could go. Trying not to cry, I headed to my room.

Our doorbell rang, and I stood at the bottom of the stairs, waiting and listening. My father answered the door and was greeted by an angry father. *Her* father had found me, and he was ready to do bodily harm. He told my father that he caught me at his home and that he's going to kill me. I could hear my father saying, "*Hold on* a minute, son…" (My father was much older, maybe by about fifteen years, and when pushed, he could be aggressive and stand his ground!) The conversation went on for about five minutes or so, and then he left with the understanding that my father would handle me and make sure that I wouldn't go to *her* house again.

A few years later, I moved and started a new life in Louisville, Kentucky, but, I never forgot those times in the neighborhood on Fifty-Sixth and Hartman. We had a blast, and I learned some valuable lessons along the way. I learned that a girl with a father in the home is like a house that has a pit bull sitting on the front porch—it can be dangerous, so you might want to act right before you enter the yard. I learned that my father could still throw the blows, and they hurt. I also learned how to control my urges and enter through the front door of a girl or woman's home with permission. And the last lesson I learned was from *her* father: when a man is present in his daughter's life, he can be an example of how a man is supposed to love and protect her. I've always wanted to go back and thank him for teaching me how a man should feel for and protect his daughter. He has been the example who showed me how to deal with boys sniffing around my own home.

#FinallyLearnedtheLesson

CHAPTER 17

Class Clown

• • •

BACK IN THE DAY IN Omaha, ninth grade was still in middle school or junior high school, which meant high school started in the tenth grade. There were several junior high schools in the local area that included seventh through ninth grades. Additionally, there was also one ninth grade center (comprised of ninth graders only). Just like any other teenager, I attended junior high with my friends. We were normal kids who enjoyed running, playing, and, of course, going to the local arcades to have fun. Back in those days, arcades were the "in" thing. I would save my lunch money and starve myself every day, and when I got home, I would eat everything in the fridge. Every day after school, we would go to the local arcade that was across the street from Nathan Hale Junior High and play video games (Pac-Man, Centipede, Ms. Pac-Man, Asteroids, Pinball, and a host of others). *My* game was Pac-Man—I could reach the level of "keys" without losing any players. We also were on the verge of adulthood and still finding our way, and many times those "ways" manifested themselves in the classroom when we came up against authority figures.

The eighth grade was particularly rough for me. I was still dealing with moving to a new neighborhood and a new school, and trying to fit in with all the new kids in the neighborhood. I played on the football team, wrestled, and was a member of the swim team. I was the only black kid on the swim team, but I learned to find a way to fit in as the season progressed. One day in class, I decided I was going to buck the system and disobey the teacher's orders. Back in those days, when instances such as these happened, the teachers could either send you to the office or give you a paddling on the spot. You *know* I wasn't about to take a paddling in class for *nobody*—you could forget that. So the alternative was to be escorted to the office where a parent would be called in lieu of the paddling and ultimately in-school suspension (I was *very* familiar with the in-school suspension program). This program was designed to keep you isolated from your peers, and you did homework only. Mr. Bartee was the *man* in that room, and *no one* wanted to see him or be near him; he had a way of making you regret whatever you did. The alternative to this was being expelled for a number of days with no chance to make up homework.

The school opted to contact my father. My father was a well-known minister in the city, and many knew him and his reputation as a no-nonsense kind of guy. I can remember the assistant principal, or school representative, speaking to my father and saying, "yes," "no," and "sure you can." A few minutes later, I saw my father traveling up the school walk. It was cold out that day, and my father wore the same type of clothing for years: a suit and tie, a pair of Stacey Adams shoes, a long trench coat, and a Russian hat—it was one of those fur hats with side flaps that could be tucked under the lip of the hat or let down to cover your ears—you couldn't tell him he wasn't sharp.

My dad asked for permission to escort me back to my classroom. Once there, he spoke to the teacher in that deep voice. "Sister _____" (he always addressed people as sister, brother, or doc-tor—he would hold that c for a small moment), "if you don't mind removing the girls from the room for a while, I'd like to talk to Marc and the boys in the class." What happened next was unprecedented. My father had me stand in the front of the class, while he sat on the teacher's desk (hat off, because he didn't believe in wearing hats inside), and he began to speak to the boys in my class. "Marc likes to be the class clooooown" (if you knew my father, he liked to extend words when he was trying to get that point across). He likes to be funny and entertain you all. Son, come over here while I'm talking—no need to stand that far away—I figure we can have a father/son act or routiiiiiiine!" Now my father, in true fashion, stood up and took off his coat, laid it across the teacher's desk and removed his *thick* belt, which had those two prongs. As he grabbed my arm and turned me around, he began to "preach" a sermon regarding class clowns. I can't remember all the words, and I certainly hope none of my friends who can help in that area are reading this. What I remember is that he grabbed me and began with, "I like to clown, too—let's see who can be the biggest clown today! Oh, you like to perform? Let's see how your friends get a kick out of this performance!" And that's about all I remember! My father calmly had me return to my seat and left the room. He told the teacher she could return and that she would have *no more* problems from me now or in the future. He tipped his hat and, as the kids would say, kept it movin'!

Later that day after being the class clown and getting a good one in front of all the boys in my class, I didn't walk to the arcade; I didn't want to be seen by the girls or walk home with the fellas—I just wanted to get to the house quick, fast, and in a hurry! I know many of you are screaming abuse right now. I know many are saying he didn't have to handle it that way; most are probably even saying that was cruel. I look back on that lesson and I can honestly say that I am happy he put it on me—grateful that the *man* never had to show me *his* type of discipline.

I learned a few lessons that day: you get it where you did it, you're held accountable for your actions, and *no one* will come to your aid when it's you or them. I learned that when you allow your children to do as they damn well please, we have a world that is described in the twenty-first century in terms of shootings, guns, gang violence, and absentee parents. I learned that an education is important and that my parents cared about that education. I learned *how* to address my own children in the twenty-first century when the time would eventually come for me to travel down this same road as a parent. I ultimately learned that there are consequences for your actions, and you'd better be ready to pay the price when you step out of line!

#FinallyLearnedtheLesson

CHAPTER 18

Joy Ride

• • •

FOURTEEN YEARS OLD, AND ONLY two words come to mind: "Raging Hormones." Did I mention that I hated church? My father, being the pastor, was always preaching, teaching, or helping others find their spiritual path; this left me a lot of time on my own to do whatever I wanted. The Sunday in question was just like any other Sunday: up early, breakfast, Sunday school, and intermission before church. Every Sunday during the intermission, my friends and I would gather around the alley of the church or on the front stairs telling stories or just enjoying each other's company. Occasionally I would sneak off and go to my aunt's house, which was around the corner from the church, and play some ball with the neighborhood kids. I would then return to church before benediction. This is the portion of the service where everyone holds hands and the pastor or one of the assistant ministers leads final song and prayer.

This Sunday, a "friend" (we won't name names to protect the *not* so inno-cent) and I were talking, and he told me that his sister said that we could take her car for a "spin." I didn't believe him and knew that he wasn't being totally honest. Again, he told me that his sister had given him permission to take the car, but there was one stipulation—he couldn't drive, but I could. Now I have six siblings (three brothers and three sisters), and my brother Anthony Louis (we call him Louie for short) would let me sit on his lap and drive. As I got older, he would allow me to drive him places when he came into town. I was more like a son than a younger brother, and he taught me a lot of things (some good and others not so good). But that's how I knew how to drive a car, and I was good. Now you know, at fourteen years old, a kid's dream is to push the whip around town with all their friends watching and them waving or chuckin' the deuces or peace sign at them from the car. So he got the keys from his sister, and off we went. You know we had to put that one finger up to signal "excuse me" as we exited the sanctuary.

So we got out to her car—I can't remember what kind of car it was—but we jumped in, started the ignition, and then we bounced. We were discussing where to go and what to do. Of course, we had this car, and there was *no one* out at this time of day because in those days almost everyone was in church, and the "spot" (Carter Lake) wouldn't jump off until well after four o'clock. I knew this *really* pretty girl—she was five feet nothing with vanilla skin, curly hair, and the most beautiful eyes a fourteen-year-old boy had ever seen. Those eyes were captivating—once they pulled you in, she was hard to resist. The chances that she was home were slim to none; you see, her father was also a prominent pastor in the city, and most preachers' kids would be in church, singing in the choir or performing usher duties (it was the life we lived—some not by choice).

So we decided to roll by her crib just for the heck of it. It wasn't a long way away from the church, and we could go there and hang out—if by chance she was home—and then get back before benediction. I knocked on her door, and to my surprise, she answered. She told me to hold on for a minute, and then she reappeared with shorts and a top on and came out on the porch. My friend's eyes lit up—as I said, she was a Vanessa Williams type with those captivating eyes—and he was pulled in hook, line, and sinker. We hung out for what seemed to be a short time talking, joking, and flirting. But eventually, it was time to go. Although my father could preach from twelve thirty to three thirty, it was always best to be back in the congregation right before benediction, so the chances of his recognizing that I wasn't there were slim. I was finally able to drag him off; however, he wanted to drive on the way back to the church (he was thirteen years old and had never been behind the wheel before, so imagine that ninety-year-old granny, hands at the nine and three, and going slower than molasses in January).

We eased our way back to the church. When we reached Twentieth and Wirt (around the corner from the church), we changed seats. I told you he couldn't drive, and there was no way he was going to parallel park that car in the same spot (if it was there). As we turned the corner onto Twentieth, moving toward

Binney Street, what we saw next made both of us yell out an explicative (I am surprised we didn't lose that bodily function on the spot) ***@#$&!*** This had never happened to me before. In ALL my days of sneaking off from the church, I had never come back after benediction. We rounded that corner and church had *already let out—everyone* was standing on the front stoop of the church! Now you can best believe that ALL eyes were on us as we pulled up, even though we were a block away! ***MOMENT OF SILENCE***

My father didn't say a word on the way home from church; he allowed me to marinate in my own juices. I sat in the backseat, and every now and again, you could see the look on his face as he peered through the rearview mirror—I knew that look all too well. My mother, *God* rest her soul, used to browbeat my father whenever I had done something; when she didn't feel up to the task of providing me with some "get right," she would fuss so much until my dad had to take action or he wouldn't get any peace or quiet. As I sat on the couch, he would give me this look as if to say, "You really done tore ya draws (old people's saying) this time." Then he would take me upstairs and lay hands on me (and not in the biblical sense). We entered the house, and my father went to change clothes (still not a word). I know enough to know that it's coming; it's only a matter of time. I can remember thinking, "*What was I thinking when I let him talk me into going? I should have just done my normal: played a li'l ball, got my li'l birdy bath, and then ran back to church as if I was there.*" My father took me to the basement to "talk." He asked me the questions, and I gave him the usual head nod and the "I don't know" shoulder shrug. He then proceeded to give me a Sunday afternoon special—one with limited words and mostly grunts!

You'd think this would have taught me a lesson, but I beg to differ—it would be a while before I learned the real lesson. That same friend, his brother, and I would take their mother's car religiously in the middle of the night for the next year or so. We would eventually tell her about those crazy days when we were in our thirties, and she would say that she always thought someone was syphoning her gas.

My father was like Homie the Clown (he didn't play that @#$&), and he believed in putting it on you so it would stick. Yet I hadn't learned the lesson as described in the last paragraph. What I learned were more lessons in accountability, to think prior to taking action, never *ever* be a follower, and, if you're going to do something illegal or on the other side of the law, make sure you can handle the consequences that go along with the "crime." In the end, it became clear that I should keep my hands off others' property and, if I wanted to drive, have a car, or be successful, it would come through hard work and no short cuts!

#FinallyLearnedtheLesson

CHAPTER 19

Be on Time

● ● ●

PRETEEN YEARS ARE HARD YEARS: your body is changing, you begin middle or junior high school, and are learning to deal with a completely new set of friends. You also have to learn to switch classes, use a locker, and, most importantly, *be on time* (before the bell)! It's that awkward time in kids' lives because they are young adults in training—more responsibility, expectations are higher, and their guardians are teaching them accountability. The *first* time I was in a position to walk to school was when I was in the ninth grade at Nathan Hale Jr. High; I was bused to all the other schools I attended prior to attending Hale. Each morning before school, we would get up, dress, eat, and head out to school. Walking or riding my bike to school was a new adventure that I readily accepted and looked forward to.

My sisters also went to Nathan Hale. On many occasions, their friends would meet them at the house, and they would all walk to school together as did my friends and I. Omaha normally had winters that started in late October and went through March of the following year, and those were the months that many of us dreaded walking to school. Most mornings, our house was the gathering spot for the group of girls who meandered around the house patiently waiting. I would normally meet the fellas on the corner, and we would start that mile trek to the school. Because of the size of our family, we *always* had a station wagon that allowed for a large number of passengers. On many occasions in the winter, I would also meander around the house, waiting to see if the old man would be playing taxi on a cold winter day. Omaha, unlike many cities in other areas of the country, didn't believe in closing schools—you had to suck it up and get ya walk on, or hope someone had mercy and gave you a ride to school.

This cold winter day everything happened as normal: the girls all arrived at my home about twenty to thirty minutes prior to the start of school, and because in those days it wasn't cool to be late, I got out my boots and got to walking. I happened to be walking to school alone, and lo and behold, the station wagon, filled with my sisters and their friends, went flying by. Anyone who knew my father *knew* he didn't believe in driving slowly anywhere—he was always on the go! As they passed me on the road, the girls all waved and laughed. My father looked and saluted me with the "old man" head nod and kept it moving; he never stopped then or *ever* to give me a ride, no matter how cold, hot, or far I was from the house. I can also remember one time in high school, I missed the city bus to Central, and I came home and asked my dad for a ride to school because I would be late if I had to wait for the next bus. Without saying a word, he finished his coffee, got dressed, and we jumped in the Monte Carlo. He then took me *back* to the bus stop and told me to get out—that the next bus should be on its way and next time, *be on time*! I used to think this dude must really hate me: he gave the girls all the benefits, yet he had me out there riding on broken bicycles (putting them together piece by piece) and walking back and forth to wherever I needed to be while he played chauffeur for the girls.

When I became a father for the second or third time (both boys), I began to do a lot of the things my father did. I was a little tougher on the boys: I made them do everything I could to ensure they were not lazy, would work at all costs, and would be productive citizens. As I look back, I started to understand that we raise our girls, showing them *how* a man should treat a woman and provide for her, and we teach our sons how to be strong and be that provider. When I look back over my life at the peaks and valleys—and ultimately my successes and failures—I *now* understand that all those days of being made to cut the grass, shovel the walk, clean the toilets, do my laundry, fold clothes, and walk to my destinations also laid the foundation for being able to depend upon self and eventually be a father and provider for my own family.

#FinallyLearnedtheLesson

CHAPTER 20

Peer Pressure

● ● ●

ON THE FIRST DAY OF practice at Shawnee High School, Coach Burks yelled, "Gimme somebody who wants to hit and is not scared!" I jumped into the left defensive tackle position and waited for the snap of the ball. I used a swim move (using my right arm under the shoulder of the offensive lineman and moving him out of the way) and got into the backfield just as the ball was being handed off to the 225-pound svelte tailback who was an all-city running back at the time. I disrupted the play and managed to bring down both the quarterback and the running back. Coach Burks blew his whistle and yelled to the lineman, "What are you doing son—is he your boyfriend? You just gonna let him come into *your* backfield?" ****SHORT PAUSE**** "Run it again!" he demanded. Again, I managed to shuck off the offensive lineman and catch the tailback as he was running full speed through the number four hole. The tailback was visibly angered that the "new" kid was able to make two plays in a row and, once off the ground, he threw the ball at me and shoved me.

The summer before that season began, June–August, I opted to return to Omaha, stay with my sister, and hang out with all my friends. The previous year I played football on the JV squad at Central High School (Eagles), and I had secretly hoped that my sister and brother-in-law would allow me to stay with them and continue my education and schooling in the city. My sister and her husband both attended Central, and I thought they would have a vested interest in me attending their alma mater. When the coach showed up to speak with them, I knew for sure I would be allowed to stay. The previous season I tried out for Central High during the summer months; they were the hardest football tryouts and practices that I had experienced. Prior to high school, I had always run the ball—and let me tell it, I was good at it; however, everything would change during tryouts at Central.

During tryouts, I was moved to the "monster" position. (The monster was the strong safety. He identified the strong side of the field and played on either side of the middle linebacker. The strong side was normally identified by the placement of the tight end.) Coach Bass worked with me to understand the concept, and he explained how to read the offense. After practice one day, I approached Coach and requested to try out for that position. In true Coach Bass fashion, he looked up at me (coach was about five feet five) and said, "What the hell you think you been doin' son?" And with that, I started my new role on the field! The JV squad at Central went undefeated in 1982, and we were favored to do some really good things in the years ahead. Unfortunately, I didn't experience any amount of success for the junior and senior years; my father had been transferred to Louisville, Kentucky, and I relocated during the Christmas break and never lived in the city again...

After the summer, I returned to Louisville and decided to try out for the team. I had missed spring training and summer workouts, and joined the team after their first win of the season; in Louisville, the season started before school. Now Shawnee was not known for being good in sports—as a matter of fact, they hadn't won a game in quite some time, and the win they experienced before I was on the team was the first in five years. I had truly gone from sugar to shit within a matter of months, but I loved the game and wanted to play—even if it was for a team that wasn't very good. After the tailback threw the ball at me, a couple of the guys gave me the proverbial pat on the back and shoulder pads to show their approval that the little 147-pound kid was able to maneuver and even hit the baddest guy on the field.

Later that evening, I made my way to the church to wait for a ride home with my father, and I was introduced to one of the female parishioners. She informed me that her daughter (who was my age) and her son both attended the same school as me and, in fact, her son should be outside to pick her up and that she would like to introduce me. Lo and behold, her son was none other than...**DRUM ROLL**...you guessed it—the tailback who earlier threw the ball at me! He greeted her with, "Yeah, Mom...we've met," and gave me the "what's up" head nod. Being the new kid coming from out of state is an extremely tough position: the girls liked me and the boys hated me—fitting in became a chore. The only way I knew how to fit in was to play football like I had learned all those years from Pop Warner to Central High. Eventually, I began to make a few friends on the team, and they started inviting me to after-school functions and parties.

Living in Omaha, I was a much more disciplined young man who had immersed himself in sports. I took pride in being healthy and not doing anything that would cause me to be less of an athlete. Even when my friends opted to try weed or drink a sip of wine or liquor, I forsook all those in the name of being an athlete. One night, after a varsity football game that we had just gotten demolished in, I accompanied the more popular players to a party at one of the cheerleader's homes. This is the first time I was allowed to hang, and there was some slow-draggin' (slow dancing in the basement), some teammates and others smoking weed, and others drinking liquor. I was offered and partook in the festivities of the evening; it was my first time drinking and smoking—and, boy, was I feeling what it was like to be on cloud nine.

I don't recall how I got home that night. I lived about fifteen to twenty miles from the school, and there were no other players on the team who lived in my area. I remember stumbling up the driveway and around to the back of the house, using my key to enter the back porch. My father's room was the closest to the back door, and he and his wife could hear me walk in and stumble into the kitchen. Anyone who has had a taste of the Mary Jane (weed) knows that it leaves you with the munchies. I entered the kitchen and rummaged through the fridge, looking for anything to eat. I finished with my snack and walked out of the kitchen into the dining room. We also had a couch in that area which was right outside my father and his wife's bedroom. I can remember stumbling over the dining room table and hitting the floor hard. My father exited the room, turned on the light, and saw me lying on the floor barely able to move. He said, "Boy, what is wrong with you—get your behind up!" I begin to mumble that I was trying to get up, but I couldn't.

My father was a former alcoholic. I can remember plenty of Sundays when he would explain that he was an alcoholic who hadn't had a drink in over twenty-plus years, so he knew the smell of alcohol and drugs. My father helped me up off the floor and had me sit on the couch in the dining room. His wife entered the room and said, "Luke, what's wrong with him?"

He responded, "He's drunk!" **Silence** My father instructed me to sleep on the couch, and we would talk in the morning.

That night, I prayed to the porcelain god more times than I care to remember and the room didn't stop spinning for what seemed to be days; it was my first night participating with my teammates, but it wouldn't be my last.

My father came to my room the following morning, sat on my bed, and began, "What happened last night? Where were you, and how did you get home?" I told my father that I hung out with the fellas after the game, we went to a party, and that's where I had something to drink. He asked if it was my first time on the "sauce" (his word for liquor), and I told him that it was my first time. I explained to my father that I was tired of not fitting in and wanted to be a part of the "in" crowd and be accepted. My father explained that making the wrong decisions can cause me a lifetime of pain, and he would rather have me think about the choices I was making before following the crowd down the path of destruction. He went on to explain that a MAN stands on his own two feet and leads the crowd where he wants them to follow. He also told me that I was not of age to continue along these lines, and that if I wanted to continue to drink and do drugs that he would not allow me to live in his home.

I didn't stop drinking or doing drugs; in fact, I increased my activity and began to be accepted by my peer group. I began to cut school, wear sunglasses to class to hide what I was doing, sell on the side, and hang out at all the parties. Eventually my father held true to his words, and my days were numbered in his home. I blamed my father for moving me from everything I knew and submerging me into the life of the unknown in the south, where some of our games had to be played during school times in certain areas because the Klan (KKK) in these parts was real. I blamed him for having to fight at school and on my way home from school, and not having any friends. I blamed him for being on a team that had only won one game in five years, and finally, I blamed him for removing me from a team of winners to move to a city that didn't even value the game of football. (Louisville was a city that loved basketball.) In 1985, my Eagle teammates won the Class A State Championship in football. I can remember talking to one of my best friends, hearing his excitement, and feeling my tears of envy that I couldn't share in that dream.

I can remember a popular TV Cheers and each time the show's theme song played I couldn't help but cry. You want be where everybody knows your name." That theme song reminded me of where I came from and what I was missing; my entire life had been turned upside down and I didn't know if I was coming or going, or what could possibly be around the bend. And the worst part was, I could hear another song ringing in my head: "Nobody loves me, nobody cares; I dream about life, but I'm livin' in a nightmare!"

My father could see the path of destruction that I was on and attempted to act as a voice in the wilderness. As a father, I now understand that each person (even your children) must make his or her own decisions. I've learned that sometimes you can show a man a better way to live and lead him to the water—but it is up to him to *decide* to drink. I've also learned that the old adage, "Raise up a child in the way he should go, and he will not depart from it," was real because although I made bad decisions and took some wrong turns in life somehow, by the grace of *God*, I ended up on the *right road*!

#FinallyLearnedtheLesson

CHAPTER 21

Race Relations

● ● ●

CRESCENT HILL IS LOCATED IN the east end of the city of Louisville. Just like Omaha, Louisville used the busing system to help integrate schools in hopes of making them more diverse and aid in bridging the gap in race relations. The area of "the Hill" where we lived was 99.9 percent white; in fact, our family was the first and only black family in this neighborhood. I lived in a predominately white area and was bused to a school in a predominately black neighborhood; in this case, busing was not working for its intended purpose. Shawnee was coined as one of the worst schools in the public school system, and the kids on the Hill were the minority when we traveled down into the West End to attend school. Oftentimes, the kids from the Hill were picked on because they came from a different ethnic background than the majority of the students who attended the school.

When my family first moved into the neighborhood, my father talked to me about the dynamics of the community and how there was a possibility that people would not be accepting of us immediately. He encouraged me to watch how I interacted with people in the area and try my best to stay out of trouble. I was raised in predominantly black communities all my life and had never experienced any racial tension, so the thought that there could be trouble had never entered my mind prior to that conversation with my father. Being the "new kid on the block"—both in the neighborhood and at the school—I was treated no differently than the other kids from the Hill who were bused to the predominantly black school who were thought to be "better" simply because of the area in which they lived and even their skin color. On several occasions on the bus ride home, kids in the neighborhood who thought I shouldn't live in their neighborhood taunted me. During my sophomore and junior years, the kids at school didn't accept me, and oftentimes I was ignored and spent a lot of time alone. I was catching it on both ends—at school and in my neighborhood.

I got off the big yellow-and-black school bus, just like every other school day, at the corner of Frankfort Avenue and Vernon Street along with two other students, who followed me toward my house. As the two students were following me, they let it be known that they were two of the people who were not happy with my being on the bus or living in *their* neighborhood. I continued to walk down Vernon, and they continued to follow, all the while taunting and throwing objects. I remained calm and I was careful not to retaliate, but a pebble hit me in the back of my neck. I was turning to confront them when I recognize my father's car pull up beside me, and he asked if I wanted a ride to the house. I responded, "No, but let me set these in here. These dudes are calling me names and throwing stuff at me." I put my books on the car's front seat, and I told my father that I was going to kick their butts. I could see my father pull down to the entrance of our driveway, exit the vehicle, and stand to see what would happen next!

I turned and confronted the would-be bullies (if they were tough enough to actually be called bullies), and we began to fight on the sidewalk next to an antique furniture store. I approached the instigator first and hit him square in the nose. I then caught the second kid, who attempted to run in the street and around the action, and I began to give him what he had begged for earlier. It was a short scuffle, and they failed to do any real damage to me during the ordeal. I walked down the street where my father was still leaning on his car. As I approached, a female neighbor, who lived across the street and witnessed the altercation, yelled to me, "Why don't you all go back to where you came from—we don't want you around here!" My father and I stood there for a few seconds, and then we got into the car and drove around to the back of our home to the garage.

We went into the house and sat at the dining room table (looking back, many lessons were taught and received at that table), and my father began to ask me exactly what happened. I explained the story, including the name-calling and taunting on the bus on our way to and from school. My father explained that he talked about these issues when we first moved into the neighborhood, and he said that he would have preferred to see me attempt to use my ability to talk my way out of a fight rather than use my fist. However, he stated that he understood that those guys crossed the line when they threw objects at me and that I didn't have to stand for being hit in any shape, form, or fashion. If I was going to teach those guys a lesson, I did it the best way by confronting them and beating them in a fair fight.

My father then confessed that he had observed the boys following and throwing objects at me and took his time driving up the street to see how I was going to handle the situation. He then confirmed that he was trying to give me a ride home to try to defuse the situation, but allowed me to handle it as I saw fit because I was the one who had to ride the bus with these guys every day for the next few years. The boys never bothered me again; I would see them from time to time at the local basketball court, and they were cordial. We rode the bus together, and they never said as much as one derogatory word after the fight. My father would use this opportunity to teach me about conflict resolution, and he indicated that he would rather I use my ability to speak to someone to resolve a problem, but he also said that it's important to know when conflict resolution means that I must defend myself and not allow others to violate my space.

I never blamed those two guys for how they treated me. I realized that it was the world that they lived in. Treating me differently because of the color of my skin was the norm in their environment. The majority of students treated them differently when they arrived on the Shawnee High Campus; therefore, they decided to take their frustrations out on me when we arrived back on "their" side of town. I believe we all learned a lesson that day on Vernon. It helped me when I enlisted in the military and helps even today. I really learned the lesson Dr. Martin Luther King lived by and my father reiterated: a *man* should be judged by the content of his character and *not* the color of his skin.

#FinallyLearnedtheLesson

CHAPTER 22

First Job

● ● ●

MY DAD CAME HOME AND put several applications on the table for me to fill out: Wendy's, McDonald's, and White Castle. He said, "It's time for you to get a job."

We lived in an area called Crescent Hill, a suburb of Louisville, Kentucky. It was comprised mostly of older Caucasian couples who were empty nesters and had lived in the area or neighborhood most of their lives. American flags draped many of the homes with well-manicured yards. The house we lived in was a church parsonage. The pastor and my dad had become good friends, and the pastor wasn't utilizing the house. He talked the board of trustees into allowing my father to stay for minimal rent. However, many of the neighborhood residents were not happy with the church's decision to rent the house to a black family.

Saturday morning, I got up early and dressed in a pair of slacks with a long-sleeved shirt and tie. It was summertime, and I can remember it was warm out that morning. I left the house and walked down the street. We lived on a dead end, but at the end of the street a long staircase led down to the street below— it was probably two stories down. I went down the stairs, took a right onto Brownsboro Road, and walked over to the Kroger. I had decided that I didn't want to use the applications my father gave me; I preferred to get my own job without help from him.

Kroger hadn't opened yet, and there was a little bench outside the main entrance to the store, so I took a seat and patiently waited. While waiting, a car entered the parking lot and then another (almost simultaneously). I observed a man exit the first car, tall in stature and on the heavy side, dressed in a suit with a tie, and probably about mid to late forties. Parked next to him I saw a woman exit her car. She wore a blue skirt with a matching blazer and heels.

They approached me as if they were going to enter the building. As they were opening the door, they observed me sitting on the bench, and the man asked if I was waiting for the store to open. I told him that I was there to see about an application and maybe even get a job. He allowed me to come into the store and sit on the bench in the front of the store.

Ten minutes or so passed, and I was invited into the main office, where I was formally introduced to Mr. David Breslin and Ms. Underwood. (I can't remember her first name.) They asked what brought me in, and I told them that I was looking for a job. They asked why I picked Kroger, and my response was that the store was close enough for me to walk to if it was warm or cold. They asked what school I attended, my hours at school, and if I played sports—if so, how would that affect my job? They also asked if there were days I couldn't work. My answers were that I could work whenever they needed me, that I played football and ran track—but that shouldn't interfere with work. I could start yesterday if they wanted, and I could most definitely work *every* Sunday if needed. I was hired on the spot by the store manager and general manager; they indicated that day that they were very surprised that I was waiting before the store opened and impressed with how articulate and confident I was during our "talk" (I didn't realize it was an interview).

My father was very happy and surprised that I was able to get a job in one day. He also told me to let them know that I needed to be off on Sundays so that I could attend church services. (*Yeah, right*—I did just the opposite; I made certain that I worked every Sunday and all day, if I could!) I worked at Kroger from 1983 until I went into the military. I attended school half days during my senior year, and worked from noon until—yes, until I couldn't work. Eventually I was moved to the night shift, where I stocked shelves and buffed floors. Kroger gave me the opportunity to begin my working career and till this day, I am forever grateful to Mr. Breslin and Ms. Underwood.

I learned that a good work ethic, persistence, being on time, and good communication skills (spoken or written) can make the difference in being considered above average or just average. I also learned that from time to time, we all need a push in the right direction. Finally, I learned that when you have been given a chance, it's your obligation to blaze a trail for those who will follow!

#LearnedVeryValuableLesson

CHAPTER 23

The Departure

● ● ●

WORKING AT KROGER PROVIDED ME with the opportunity to learn the value of money, the importance of saving, and the drive to climb the ladder of success. I had recently moved from Crescent Hill to the West End. The West End was about ten miles from the old neighborhood, and there were buses (TARC, or Transit Authority of River City) that ran until about midnight that I would take back to the old neighborhood. This was a significant move for me because my job was located in the old neighborhood. I had become a senior bagger and was making all the hours and overtime a young sixteen- or seventeen-year-old could ask for. Everything I had grown accustomed to was on the Hill; moving and readjusting was going to be hard.

As a bagger, my duties included bagging groceries for customers, taking customers' groceries to their vehicles, cleaning aisle spills, making sure the entry to the store was clean and dry (especially during rainy days), and retrieving carts from the parking lot. One day while retrieving carts, I had to go next door, which happened to be a bank. Seeing the bank gave me an idea that I should have an account and start saving money; so I planned to go and speak to someone because I had no idea where to start. I eventually opened checking and savings accounts and received my very first ATM card (I was big-time now).

We moved to Date Street, which was located not too far from downtown Louisville and not too far from my father's church. We were in the heart of the city and in a predominantly black part of town. It was a totally different atmosphere than I had become accustomed to. I had everything I needed within walking distance from my previous house, so the move was not well received by me! Every day I caught the bus from my school (Shawnee)—which was even farther into the West End (about twenty blocks)—to my job. Then, around 11:00 p.m., I caught the TARC to Twenty-Second and Market and walked about ten blocks to Date Street.

My female friend who lived on the Hill often allowed me to drive her car, or she took me home from work when she could. On the day in question, the plan was for me to drive her car to work. After I got off, I would pick her up, and she would take me home. She owned a white Pinto; it wasn't the best little car, but it was able to get you from point A to point B. On my way into work, I was looking in the rearview mirror at some girls I had just passed by, and I inadvertently *hit* a parked car (the car was owned by my supervisor)! The police were called, and my friend, her mother, and grandmother came to the store to see the damage. Everyone was calm and very supportive, and they worked with me to get everything sorted out without further incident. Because my shift had started, and I was worried about getting off in time to catch the last bus back down to the West End, my friend's grandmother said that I could just come to her house after work, spend the night, and then catch the school bus (the one I rode prior to moving from the Hill) to school. She assured me that she would contact my father to let him know what happened (I figured it would be easier coming from her) as soon as she got home.

The next day at school, my little sister approached me and asked, "Where were you last night?" I told her the story and that Granny (my friend's grandmother) called Daddy to let him know what happened. My sister said, "Evidently she didn't—Daddy told me to tell you if I saw you to NOT come home, and you can get your stuff off the back porch in a garbage bag." Now back in the day, I was filled with pride and, because my home life wasn't the best, and I really didn't want to be there, I decided to pick up my belongings as requested. I could have called my dad and taken the ticket I received from the incident to show him as proof, or I could have asked Granny to contact my father and explain, as promised, the prior evening's events. I decided that this was the *perfect* opportunity for me to leave and try this thing called life on my own. So I took the bus over to Date Street, where my father came out to the back porch and watched as I gathered my belongings (my father never gave idle threats; he meant what he said and said what he meant), and I headed to the Hill.

I would spend the next three or four months sleeping in abandoned cars, sleeping at different friends' homes on their couches, and taking quick showers at those same friends' homes after their parents departed for work and before the bus came for school. I recall a time one night sleeping in an abandoned car behind my female friend's home, and I began to pray. I promised God that if I ever made it out of this situation, I would always make sure other children like me would never have to live from house to house or in abandoned cars.

I never lived in my father's home again. The tension between us had finally come to a head, and things would never be the same for as long as he would live.

I learned several lessons from this time in my life. I learned that if you can't or don't want to live by the rules of others, you have to get your own, so you can live the way you want. I also learned that rushing to adulthood will have you wishing that childhood could last forever. Finally, I also understood that *everything* happens for a reason, and if you're blessed to live long enough, you just might understand *both* sides of the coin. As a man and a father, I now understand the "flip side of the coin" and feel that I am equipped to *teach* the lessons that I have learned from going through my storm.

#FinallyLearnedtheLesson

CHAPTER 24

Rightfully Mine

● ● ●

Living with Granny, I began to learn about being an adult and taking on responsibilities such as learning to drive, managing bank accounts, saving money, and paying bills. Granny and I had become roommates and, because she was elderly and lived on a fixed income, I had begun to learn from her how much it cost to live. Granny couldn't see very well and, on many occasions, her cataracts would hinder her from seeing even with glasses, so I became her eyes. I would take her to the bank, and I made sure she withdrew the correct amount of money from her accounts. I wrote out her checks, and sometimes even signed them. I took her shopping, and many days did the shopping for her and her friends (she had a young helper and didn't mind sharing me with her friends). I acted as her personal chauffeur, and we got along, most times, famously.

I worked every day making $3.35 per hour, minimum wage at the time (many will probably recall that this was *not* a lot of money—I think I still may have a check stub or two), which was not enough to help with costs associated with my food, utilities, gas to mow the lawn, or any of the other necessities required to live a decent life. When my mother passed, my father became eligible to receive social security payments on behalf of my two sisters and me. I can remember overhearing conversations in different settings about the money he was receiving, and that's how I knew it existed. After trying to figure out a way to continue to live and make more money, I thought of a good way to make ends meet and continue to go to school every day—all without having to get a second job! I decided that the money my father received on my behalf was not being utilized for me to live, but only for him and those who continued to live in his house; it was *not* beneficial to me and therefore, I should have a right to the money.

I would devise a plan on how to get the money from my father. I *knew* he wasn't going to give me the check, and he wasn't the type of person to give *money* of any kind away—even if it wasn't his. So I researched where the money came from, why any surviving offspring would get the money, and how to get the money to come to me. I started by going to the downtown Louisville public library, then I made calls to different agencies, and I spoke with some of the older guys on my shift about what I wanted to do. Everyone had a theory, but things weren't adding up. I eventually spoke with someone who could help (can't remember the name), made an appointment, and went in to talk about my options. I was informed that I didn't have a right to the money, that because my father was the legal guardian, I could not have it changed to a different address. I inquired further and spoke to two people in the office, including the office supervisor. They explained that although they could not change the address on the checks, what they could do (and what had been done previously) was to send a letter in the mail requesting that my father or guardian reply or come in for a meeting to determine who should get the check. If there is no response within a specified time, the check would then be cut to me and sent to my address.
THINKING

So I went home and thought long and hard about how to get what I believed was mine without having to outright fight my father for the money. I then decided that I would go to his home every day to check the mail and confiscate the letter. At this time, I had only three classes in school: my last class was co-op. Co-op was designed to help people get jobs, and the class was also designed to teach students how to manage money by developing a budget and learning to write checks. Because I already had a job, I would leave school early every day and still received credit because I would report to work. On my way back to the East End, I would stop by my father's house and check the mail. if the letter carrier hadn't arrived, I would normally wait for the mail delivery. About a week later, I stopped by my father's house and, lo and behold, the letter had arrived. I took the letter, held on to it, and he was none the wiser.

The following month I received the check, and I began to use it to help make ends meet for Granny and myself. A few months later, my father called and inquired about the check. He asked if I had received it and then began to question me about how I was able to get it changed from his house. I told him about how I went down to the office and had the letter sent to his home. I then took the letter so that he couldn't respond. **SILENCE** My father slowly asked if I gave Granny any money to help her around the house. I explained that I needed the money to help Granny and me make ends meet. He said that was good, that it could help make things easier for us, and to call him if I needed anything. I was actually surprised that my father found out the truth and was not angry with me for getting the money through deceit. I was even more surprised that he inquired as to the use of the money and then offered to assist even further if needed. As I replay that day in my mind, I believe my father knew that I needed and deserved the money if I went to such extremes to obtain it.

I learned that sometimes even parents understand that desperate times call for desperate measures. I learned that my father knew that I was entitled to the money that he was using to pay bills in a home where I no longer lived, and I learned that although the method was less than honest, he was proud that I figured out a way to make it work. My father would later boast and brag about my accomplishments. I always said that he didn't do anything to help me on my journey. But now, I have finally learned that he taught me many lessons along the way and had become directly and indirectly responsible for many of my accomplishments—*even* if it was only because I wanted to prove that I could make it without his help!

#FinallyLearnedtheLesson

CHAPTER 25

Common Courtesy

● ● ●

MY FATHER WAS THE FIRSTBORN of Reverend SilKirtis and Adglee Nichols, born in 1927, in Chicago, Illinois. His parents were from Mississippi and Arkansas, and he often told how he had a southern upbringing in the city of Chicago. My father often told stories to my siblings and me, and many we found out during his sermons—about his upbringing during the Great Depression where they literally didn't know where their next meal was coming from, and how his family survived off eating nothing more than onion soup for days at a time. My father was certainly "old school"; he made no bones about how he was raised in a Christian home with strong values, coupled with a stint in the US Army during the Korean War, which helped mold him into the stern disciplinarian and waste-not-want-not man he had become.

My parents raised us to say "yes, sir," "yes, ma'am," "no, sir," "no, ma'am," and the like. If you were in my father's presence and you said "yeah" or "nah," that could be cause for you to seek medical attention. He found that very disrespectful for a child to address an adult in that manner and, on many occasions, he used sir and ma'am to address people his junior—no matter the race! Many in the community believe that these are old slave terms used to control blacks and keep them in line. My father believed that the terms were respectful, and we would use them because he said we would—*period*! My father also had other beliefs such as a man not wearing a hat or cover inside any building.

I can remember having a couple of friends over to the house when I was thirteen or fourteen years old, and my father walked in. The fellas and I were standing in the kitchen drinking Kool-Aid, and my father said to my partner, "Son, is it raining in the house?" We all looked around, and my friend said no. My father repeated, "No...no what?" He repeated, "No, it's not raining outside." I knew it was a wrap at that point; my friend had no idea that he was on the edge, and I could do nothing to save him. Many of my friends didn't like to hang around much because my father would always ask the standard questions:

1. What church do you attend?
2. Are you going this Sunday?
3. Ask your parents can you come with us.
4. What're your parents' names and number?

So as my friend was looking for leaks in the ceiling, my father told him to remove his hat while he was in the house and that common courtesy dictated that he should only wear a hat while outside a building. He THEN addresses the word no—he explains to my partner that the word "no" should always be followed with a sir or ma'am here at 4210 North Thirty-Sixth Street, and that when he (my father) asks another question, he better hear it...

Years later, we had moved to Louisville, Kentucky, and I was no longer living with my father; I was seventeen and technically living on my own because I couldn't abide by the rules of the house. I received a phone call from my sister, letting me know that my paternal grandmother and Uncle Joe were in town for the weekend and wanted to see me before they were to depart on Monday. My grandmother (Adglee), was one of the sweetest, kindest people in the world; she was very soft-spoken and had that down south, country way of speaking, using words like chile (child) and babee (baby). You had to listen very carefully so that you could hear all the words that she would use, or you could miss some because her voice was so light.

So I decided that I would attend church (my father's family was very religious: his father was a pastor, two of his sisters were married to ministers, and my uncle Joe and aunt Dorothy both sang in gospel choirs for as long as I can remember). So going to church was the best way to ensure that I had an opportunity to see my grandmother before she left. I attended church, and afterward had an opportunity to speak with my grandmother and uncle. At some point during the conversation, my grandmother asked if I would be coming to the house to eat and spend a little more time. I agreed, and headed to my father's home for Sunday dinner. We all gathered in the living room, talking and having fun, and suddenly my father entered the room and asked me to come outside so that he could speak to me away from the family. We went outside, exited the front porch, and stood on the sidewalk in front of the house. My father explained to me that I had failed to speak to his wife when I entered *their* home, and he went on to say that I could either go back inside and speak, or I could remove myself from the premises.

As I was walking away, my grandmother exited the home, came down the steps, and said, "Honey, where ya going?" My father answers that I was leaving and never missed a stride as he returned up the steps and into the house. My grandmother came down to the sidewalk and asked me what that was all about. I explained that I failed to speak when I came in and she (father's wife) got mad, and now *he* put me out and said I couldn't come back in. She said, "Babee, go on in there and talk to ya daddy." I told her that he ain't trying to hear what I have to say; he'd just rather be with "her," and they just want me out of the way. Grandmother looked at me hard, gave me a hug, and said she would be praying for me.

My father was a man of principle. He believed in saying "sir" and "ma'am," children acting accordingly, obeying your parents and, most of all, being respectful. Years later, when I became a parent, my daughter was attending private school at Mount Zion Christian Academy, and each week they received a Bible verse and had to recite it in front of the class. I can recall helping my daughter with it before and after track practice. This particular Bible verse was Ephesians 6, and many times, they would have it written in a manner a child could understand: **"Children, obey your parents; honor your mother and father, and your days will be long upon the face of the earth."** We practiced this verse for four days straight because she just wasn't getting it. I would get frustrated with her, and I had to take small breaks because I just couldn't figure out why she could remember the lyrics to a song in third grade, but not this simple Bible verse.

As I look back over this story, I told my grandmother that "he put me out, and I can't come back in," which was not true. My father actually gave me an opportunity to go back in and speak as I entered *her* home. Pride wouldn't allow me to go back, use common courtesy, and speak to the homeowner. My grand-mother lived to see ninety-six years old; we celebrated her birthday in April of 2003, and she passed before her ninety-seventh birthday. My father lived to be eighty-six years of age, and each had lived a fruitful life. And as I look back at that Bible verse that *I never forgot*, I realized that the lesson wasn't for my daughter. She couldn't understand or learn it because it wasn't for her to learn. It was *mine* to learn, *mine* to understand, and *mine* to recognize its value and the error of my ways. I believe that God was working through her to reach me.

Today, in my "tool" bag, I use the words "yes, sir," "yes, ma'am," "no, sir," and "no, ma'am." I don't enter a home or building with my hat on; when I enter a room, I *always* speak to those who are already in the room; and I most certainly always speak when I enter someone else's home. Because of his principles and beliefs, my father wouldn't allow me to disrespect his home or his wife that day, as she was the lawful owner of the home—no matter how hard it was for him to turn away from me—it allowed me to learn the lessons in my own time.

I learned that being courteous is not limited to parents, elders, or family members—it pertains to *anyone* whom you deal with in life; it is also in line with the "golden" rule, "Do unto others as you would have them do unto you."

#FinallyLearnedtheLesson

CHAPTER 26

The Future

● ● ●

ONCE I MOVED TO LOUISVILLE, I was given placement exams to determine where I was in the Louisville public school system. It's important to note that I had legally failed the eighth grade while at Nathan Hale Junior High back in Omaha but was allowed to "pass"; whether I would continue on to the ninth grade or be placed back in the eighth depended on the first semester of ninth grade. I attended Central High School prior to leaving Omaha. Central was more of a college preparatory school and, quiet as it's kept, I hadn't excelled there as a student. I actually struggled to keep up with the rest of my classmates.

When we arrived in Louisville, I was in the second semester of tenth grade, and my first class was math (algebra) with Mr. Kincaid. He reminded me of Michael Gross from the cast of *Family Ties*. Mr. Kincaid asked me to show him in the book where I was before I left Omaha. I had already finished the book that they were using, and he had me take a quick test that I eventually aced. I was removed from his regular algebra class and registered in honors math (looking around...who me—the kid who had *never* excelled in academics?). Eventually, I was moved to all honors classes for the remainder of my time in high school. I finished the tenth grade and did pretty well. My grades were up, and I was starting to believe that perhaps I was an honor roll student and had the capability to hang with the smart kids. Unfortunately, all new experiences are not all peaches and cream, and some bad always goes along with the good.

My junior and senior years were not much different than the completion of my sophomore year. I was still considered the new kid on the block, which normally didn't go over with the males; however, the females didn't seem to mind that there was a new kid on the block and therefore, I gravitated toward them as potential friends. Shawnee High School was located in the infamous West End in Louisville; it was known at that time as one of the WORST schools in the public school system. The *huge* school covered a city block in width, three full blocks in length, and was three stories high. It also had an Olympic-size pool and was easily the largest school I had attended and probably with the worst student body (as many would have you believe)!

There are always those who aid in shaping and molding you into the person you will eventually become, and I, like every impressionable teenager, was no exception to that rule. Mr. Peacock, my honors class English teacher, was a 1980s modern hippie with his rather long, dirty-blond hair that was cut short on the sides and had that Elvis Presley-looking front rock stars would wear back in the day. He was an excellent teacher and would challenge the class every day with teaching us how to convey a message via written and verbal communication. I give credit to Mr. Peacock for affording me the opportunity to learn how to communicate with those who didn't come from the same background as I and perhaps had a better grasp of the English language. There was also Ms. Price, my only black teacher my three years at Shawnee. As a football player at the school, I realized that others would label me as a "dumb jock." I was the *only* male in Ms. Price's typing class; I believe that she thought I was only there in the beginning because I felt it was an easy class. The real reason I took typing was multifaceted:

* I didn't like working with my hands in classes like wood shop or mechanics.
* Who wanted to be around a bunch of dudes—I already played sports and had to be around them all day.
* I always thought typing would come in handy someday as I moved into the workforce.

After a few weeks, I began to excel in Ms. Price's class. She saw that I was catching on fast and beginning to type with fewer mistakes; I was slowly becoming one of her star students. Not everything was as it seemed. Ms. Price somehow found out about some of the things I had gotten myself into as a "follower" or because of being the new kid and attempting to fit in—"peer pressure"—if you will. In the neighborhood and in school, I began to hang out with different types of friends, and those friends were drinkers and often did drugs. I began to use drugs and drink as well (all along knowing it was not who I was or what I was supposed to be doing; I knew better). I began to skip classes and wear sunglasses in school to hide what I had been doing when we snuck off school property. I also began to make a few extra bucks by selling to other students during school hours. Ms. Price began to take a larger interest in my behavior outside her classroom, and one day confronted me about my recent activity. She asked me into her classroom late one evening after class and began to speak with me about my behavior. She stated that of *all* her students, I was special. I was different from the other boys she observed walking the hallways—different from my teammates on the football team. She indicated that she *knew* that I was raised differently and that it was something I couldn't hide—no matter how hard I tried to fit into that lifestyle, it wouldn't work!

Mr. Chick Langness (yes, *his* first name was Chick) was my honors sociology/psychology teacher. He was a very tough teacher who would use social issues to challenge our beliefs. There were two very vivid lessons that I walked away with from his class. The first lesson was an assignment he had given that was based on real news stories, and in the eighties, one of the largest stories in the news that year was the New York vigilante. On a New York subway, during an altercation between a group of four or five black teenagers and a white man, the white man—who felt threatened by the teens—shot the young black men. Our assignment was to argue one side versus the other. Most of my classmates were white females, and if memory serves me correctly, we had maybe six white males and three black females. I was the only black male in the class, and the discussion made me very uncomfortable. I was selected to argue the side of the white male and give my thoughts and opinions on why he could be right for defending himself. Being a black male, it was hard for me to put myself in the perpetrator's shoes. But, I managed to make good arguments on his behalf. The second lesson was about sociological imagination, which is the ability to see things socially and understand how they interact and influence each other. To have a sociological imagination, a person must be able to pull away from the situation and think from an alternative point of view; it requires "thinking ourselves away from our daily routines and looking at them anew." To acquire

knowledge, it is important to break free from the immediacy of personal cir-
cumstances and put things into a wider context, rather than following a routine.

I had begun to enjoy school. I was excelling and making new friends who
had all been talking about college and their plans for the next journey in life. I
began to think that I, too, could be a college student. Public speaking and talking to people interested me the most. I had grown to *love* psychology and wanted
to work with people, so I began the process of looking at schools. Of course,
I wanted to play football at the next level and, like all the other seniors on my
team, I had started getting information from different colleges and invitations
to officially visit the campuses. Due to my being semiemancipated, I was on my
own to try to "figure out" how to attend college; I began to respond to schools
and set up visits to find out more about schools and what it would take to attend.
After my first official visit, I was hooked—I wanted to experience the college
life and learn more. I had experienced a small portion of what college work
could entail; I may have failed to mention that my sociology/psychology classes
were college-accredited courses based on a curriculum from the University of
Louisville. I felt I had what it took to attend at the next level.

One day I visited my father with this great plan to attend college. He understood
the magnitude of a college education, but was always concerned with the cost
associated with sending a child to school. So we had a conversation at the living
room table and I told him about my college visit, the campus, how far away it
was, and what I wanted to study. We talked about transportation, the football
team, and how much, if any, the school would pay for me to be there. I really
didn't understand how athletic scholarships worked. I was under the impression
that if you were a good athlete and you met all the requirements, you received
a letter from the coach or staff that you were going to receive a scholarship
to attend that college or university. However, after reading the fine print and
becoming more familiar with the process, I found that I would be responsible
for many of the costs associated with attending secondary school. My father,
although happy that I was interested in school, made it very clear that he didn't
have the financial means to send me to school, nor would he be taking out a
loan or signing any documents for Pell Grants or any other tuition assistance. If
I were going to go to college, I would bear all the financial responsibility on my

shoulders. I approached my father three different times with regard to signing documents needed to apply for school, and each time he stood his ground—he would be unable to help me realize my dream and would not put himself in a financial bind to aid in that endeavor. I graduated high school in June of 1985 and, after high school, I meandered around the city of Louisville working at Kroger, hanging out with friends, doing drugs, and living the party life. I would blame my father for many years for failing to give me guidance or financial support and for everything I hadn't accomplished in my life.

I learned that becoming a *man* was not going to be easy, and that if you don't believe in yourself—*no one else* will, either. I learned that even those who are not connected to you as family members can take an interest in you and invest in your life, and not all investments will have monetary value. I learned to look at both sides of a coin, try to argue on both sides of the fence, and make a decision based on the facts and not only emotion—or based on the color of my skin. I learned that sometimes the *only* person you can or should count on is yourself. My father taught me a very valuable lesson during those days at the table—no matter how many points I brought up, he was not in a financial position to send me to school, and he wasn't willing to risk taking out loans or signing documents that would make him legally responsible for any payments in the future. The main lesson I learned was that "if it's to be, then it would be up to me," and that before I had children, I wanted to make certain that I would be in a position to support them in every aspect of their lives and help them attain their goals. It made me work harder to secure a better life, for I *knew* that I didn't want to live in the manner that I had during my high school years.

#FinallyLearnedtheLesson

Graduation

● ● ●

I CAN REMEMBER RUSHING DOWNTOWN in my little white Audi that barely ran without having to fix it at every other stop light. It was 1985, and I was set to graduate that morning from Shawnee High School. I didn't have much of a support system; I only had my immediate family, and I wasn't sure if they would be there—but I darn sure wanted to walk across that stage after the last two and a half years that took place and hopefully start a new life. At the end of junior year, we began to prepare for senior year, which included a variety of requirements: taking SAT/ACT examinations, purchasing a cap and gown, taking senior pictures, going on senior trip, going to the prom, electing officers, and ordering class rings. Because I was technically on my own, I had an abundance of documents I had to sort through and try to figure out how to make all the right decisions.

One of the last days of junior year, the rising senior class was required to meet on the first floor in a large room. I was not sure why we had to meet there because I often didn't pay attention in class or listen to the announcements over the PA system. I followed my classmates to the designated meeting area. I observed several suit jackets with shirts and bow ties on one portable clothes rack, and next to it another rack with women's gowns. Each student was made to put on his or her size and take a quick photo. I soon realized that we were taking our class pictures, and I remember thinking I'd hate to be the person who has to put this shirt and jacket on after me; I wore a juicy Jheri curl back in those days, and normally a collar shirt would need dry cleaning after being worn.

After pictures were taken, we immediately were ushered to see a Balfour Rings representative who was equipped with a brochure of all their products. I loved jewelry, and it didn't take long for me to open the brochure and fantasize about the ring I wanted. Balfour had a variety of rings for sale, including allowing the customer an opportunity to customize his or her own ring. I envisioned my ring with a thick gold band with a football engraved on one side and my jersey number thirty-two on the adjacent side. After adding all the "extras" I wanted, the price of the ring came up to a whopping $300 bucks. I would soon reach out to my father to discuss money for graduation pictures, cap and gown, and, of course, a class ring. My father looked at all the information and explained that he didn't have any money to give me for any of the aforementioned items on the graduation list. However, he told me that he could afford to provide me with the $30 down payment for the ring; I would have to get the balance on my own.

I worked a meager part-time job that didn't provide a lot of money. But I knew that I had enough time to save for the ring I wanted (I wasn't exactly sure about the other items, but that ring was to die for), so I devised a plan to save as much money as I could in order to get this ring by the due date. I began to work extra hours to afford the ring, pictures, and fees for the required examinations for college. I accepted an overnight position buffing floors and stocking shelves in an effort to help defer the cost (night work was a 35 percent increase in pay coupled with a higher hourly rate). I would save money for the summer and through the following school year so that I could pay my fees. I eventually paid my own fees to include the balance of $270 for my personally designed high school ring.

I entered the auditorium, and my classmates had already lined up and were ready to enter and take their seats for the beginning of the ceremonies. I hurried to put on my cap and gown and find my place in the line prior to entering the auditorium and proceeding to our seats. I don't recall much—I was out late with many of my classmates, drinking the night prior—and the ceremony is a total blur. After the ceremonies, I was shocked to see my younger sister and my father standing in the back of the auditorium: they said their congratulations; we made small talk, and then we went our separate ways. I always wondered what it would have been like to graduate with my original friends, have my family make a big fuss about coming to my graduation, throwing me a party, receiving envelopes filled with money, or at the least, filling out graduation invitations with wallet-size photos. None of those things would happen for me; I was only able to get a few pictures and the ring—there would be no fanfare, no envelopes…no large crowd screaming for me when my name was called.

For many years, I looked back on this part of my life with bitterness, jealousy, and envy for those who had those types of experiences. I would remain angry with my father for uprooting me at a very vulnerable stage in my life. I had, for many years, continued to look in the rearview mirror, which would become fuel for my anger. Twenty-five years later, I was blessed to have the opportunity to fund my daughter's graduation: she had the ring and the graduation pictures. We worked on scholarships together, we did college visits, we filled out all the paperwork, we rented tables and chairs along with the inflatable jump machines, we funded all the food, and there was a huge crowd to shout, scream, yell, and blow whistles when she crossed the stage. When we first set out to have a party with all the extras, I remembered my story and I certainly wanted her to experience something memorable that she could always look back on and smile; so I never had an issue with providing much of the money required to make certain it was memorable.

However, after I looked back over the hills and the valleys, I finally had to recognize that I wasn't supposed to have the fanfare, the big crowd, the expensive pictures or the extravagant parties. Maybe, just maybe, I had to go through this storm so that I would understand the value of special occasions and work that much harder for them to come to fruition for someone else. I believe with ALL my heart that everything happens for a reason, and God knew that someday I would remember my own pain and spare those that I love. I finally got the fanfare, the pictures, the scholarship, and the money-filled envelopes. When I was able to step back and see the large picture that *hot* June day in 2010, I could finally see that I would share in her joy just as much as I would have twenty-five years earlier!

#FinallyLearnedtheLesson

CHAPTER 28

Premonition

● ● ●

I WAS EIGHTEEN YEARS OLD and had not lived in my father's home for almost two and a half years. I was working at Kroger (a southern grocery store chain) on the night shift, buffing floors and stocking shelves. At this time of my life, I had been living with my friend's grandmother, who was known affectionately as Granny. Her name was Ora Mae Holiday; she was a neighborhood icon who I believe was sent by *God* to watch over me in my hour of need. Granny took me in after I departed my father's home. She lived in what would be called a one-bedroom shotgun house. The small home was normally greater in length than width. If I had to guesstimate, I would say the living space was no more than eight hundred square feet.

My father, who kept in touch with me by phone, would also make the occasional trips to Stoll Avenue (Granny's home) to check on my activities and whereabouts and to make sure I was still alive and doing halfway decent. My friends and I at Kroger were typical teenagers who loved to party every night after work; we would go out to clubs, smoke, pop pills, drink, drive fast cars, and chase even faster women. I also had my neighborhood homies I hung with; we would do the same things as my Kroger buddies; however, we played cards (tonk or twenty-one) most weekend nights. My father had this thing: some called it an ability to see the future, many said *God* would show things to him, and others said he was clairvoyant (this is the ability to see the future)...

Until the age of thirteen, I lived at 4210 North Thirty-Sixth Street, Omaha, Nebraska, best explained as down the street from North High School and only two blocks from one of the larger hospitals in the city, Immanuel Hospital. Back then, it was a busy facility and there was always something going on, whether it was regular appointments, *babies being born, or the emergency room filled with drive-in patients or those who came by ambulance. One Sunday morning, my three sisters and I were all coming down for breakfast, and my father was saying that one of the church members had passed during the night. My older sister asked who called him this morning to let him know. She also made it clear that she didn't hear a phone ring (of course, back in those days we didn't have text, IM, cell phones, or pagers), and the normal way of communicating would have been with a regular home phone. My father said that no one called; he felt her spirit as it departed the earth, and she visited him prior to her ascending. I can remember my sisters and I looking at each other and communicating without words (saying yeah, right). Not one minute later the phone rang, and the woman's family member informed my father that this particular parishioner has passed. **silence***

Early Monday morning, June 10, 1985, my father called me. We made small talk, and my father asked me what I was doing, how I was living, what I was into, and what I had planned for the upcoming few days. I told him that I was up to nothing but work and hanging out with my friends, doing the normal. My father got very serious, and he told me about a dream that he had the night prior. "Marc, I had a dream last night and it bothered me all day Sunday, before my sermon, after church, all night last night, and even till today. I called to tell you that you need to be careful—stay in the house for a few days and watch the company you keep…

It's amazing how genes work: some brothers and sisters act alike, many look alike, or you can see one in a store and then another on a completely different side of the store and know they are related. I can recall my number two brother, Anthony (Louie), visiting our house when I was about six or seven years old, and he was having a conversation with my mother and older sister. I was "sleep" on the couch. I can remember my brother saying that I looked just like my eldest brother Richard (Ricky), and that I was a dead ringer for him…

My father went on to tell me that in his dream he received a phone call and that he was informed his son was killed. Later in the dream, when he opened the casket, it was *my face* that he saw, and for the *first* time in his life that fear had overcome him. He was adamant about my laying low and being cautious throughout the week. He went on to say that he would be in a revival in Detroit and would return the following week. June 14, 1985, was a Friday I will never forget: I had gone out the previous night as usual—failing to heed my father's warning, blowing it off as just a dream with no merit whatsoever. My paternal grandmother, who lives in Chicago, Illinois, Adglee Thompson, called me to inform me that my oldest brother (Ricky) was killed in Wichita, Kansas, **SILENCE** I fell to my knees and cried for what seemed an eternity; I realized that the dream was not about me. The message was *not* for me; it was for my brother—my father mistook one for the other. My mind went immediately to the times my father had a premonition and we didn't believe him. I don't know if my brother would have heeded the warning any more than I did, but I believe that all things work out the way that they are designed. We buried my first sibling a few days later next to my mother in Omaha, Nebraska, at Forest Lawn Cemetery.

I sometimes wonder if *God* allowed me to receive the "message" so that I would know that his gifts are real and are not to be mocked, as I had done on several occasions in the past. I realized that my father's faith in *God* was real and his never-wavering obedience to the Most High would someday be witnessed to in a manual or book! I learned that *all* things are possible through Christ, even if we are too blind to see it or not wise enough to believe it, yet open-minded enough to receive it!

#FinallyLearnedtheLesson

CHAPTER 29

A New Beginning

● ● ●

THERE WAS A SNOWSTORM THE previous night and it was still snowing; everything was darn near shut down and the ice was starting to form under the snow, making driving conditions even worse. If this kept up, I was never going to make my appointment! I had been working at Kroger for the better part of three years. I was a regular on the night crew, where my job consisted of buffing floors and stocking shelves. When I first started working at the store, it closed around eleven on weekdays and midnight on weekends; soon we were going to a twenty-four-hour operation, and many of us were not happy about the change.

When I came into work, the first thing I had to do was block off the first three aisles. The aisles were set up from right to left, with aisle one starting in the produce area and working your way left to the milk and eggs. I would guesstimate that there were about nineteen or twenty aisles total, and my job was to finish it in a timely manner and then begin stocking product onto the shelves. There were about twelve guys working the night shift: most of them were grown men with families, and I was the youngest on the crew. I had a chance to watch and learn from each of these guys, all of whom came from different walks of life, yet all ended up in the same store, working the night shift, performing the task of restocking shelves so they might look neat and well-kept for customers. Additionally, the stockers were also responsible for ordering items prior to their being sold out; we never wanted an item to be completely gone before we reordered.

My job was fun: buffing floors gave me the opportunity to move around, talk to the different guys in the aisle, and hear their likes, dislikes, troubles, and concerns. But most of all, it gave me an opportunity to learn what types of music they liked. Each stocker had one or two aisles assigned to him (at this time there were no female stockers), and he brought his own boom box or radio to work. I could go down an aisle and hear country music, "I got oceanfront property in Arizona" bellowing out, and in another aisle I might hear rap, "Friends...how many of us have them, Friends...ones we can depend on, let's be friends!" In another aisle they may have bluegrass playing, and then on to honky-tonk, blues, and jazz. I learned a lot about music and those who listened to it. After buffing, I had to start stocking shelves in the frozen food aisles. I hated working frozen foods; it required me to go into the freezer (dressed warm with gloves) and then stock the freezers for customers. I certainly found out that this wasn't something that I wanted to do for the rest of my life. My girlfriend asked me to consider a life in the military. After considering this option, I decided to speak with a recruiter about the US Air Force and see what they had to offer. I eventually took the Armed Services Vocational Aptitude Battery (ASVAB) and scored well enough to enter into the Delayed Entrance Program—which required that you wait to enter the military for a particular job, which was normally six months.

As I stated, everything was darn near closed down and the city buses weren't even running, so I had to call the one person who I *knew* could drive in the rain, sleet, or snow. My dad pulled up to the apartments on Zorn Avenue and waited at the bottom of the hill for me to come down (too much ice to climb the hill). Once in the car, my dad and I had a conversation about my signing up (he had just found out that day that I was on my way to basic training). He asked if I was sure that this was what I wanted to do, what my job would be, and where I was going for basic training. This would be the last time I spoke to my father for some time. I was shipped off to Lackland Air Force Base in San Antonio, Texas, on a cold and snowy Valentine's Day in 1986. Thus began a new journey, one that changed the course of my life forever.

Working at Kroger was a good learning experience that taught me a good work ethic, how to interact with people, and the importance of being on time. I learned that I didn't want to stock shelves or buff floors the rest of my career. I learned that if I wanted to have the finer things in life, I might have to reach higher. I also learned that you can't be afraid to move forward, leaving once familiar things behind. My father once told me when I was a little boy (which continues to prove his "psychic" ability), "When you go into the army, you will understand sacrifice." I never did understand this saying; perhaps he meant that the world didn't revolve around me, and that one day I would understand the big picture and how I fit in.

#FinallyLearnedtheLesson

CHAPTER 30

Revelation

● ● ●

My first duty station in the US Air Force was Kadena Air Force Base in Okinawa, Japan, also known as "the *Rock*"! The Rock was an island approximately seventy miles long and seven miles wide at its widest point. While on the Rock, I met some great friends whom I still keep in contact with twenty-nine years later. We were a close-knit group who often gathered at each other's homes for holidays, BBQs in the summer, card parties, and sightseeing on the island. I lived on Camp Courtney, which was a marine-run base. On this base, there were several eight-story, high-rise apartment buildings designed for soldiers with families, and fortunately for me, the marines didn't have enough enlisted members who had families to take advantage of the newly built high-rises. The apartments were one-thousand-square-foot, three-bedroom, two-bath living quarters with a kitchen, dining room, and living room. In 1988, these were state-of-the-art living quarters, and a young airman was lucky to be allowed to live there.

This night, about fourteen of my closest friends came by for an evening of fun. We often played our music loud (everyone had a nice system with the best speakers), grilled on the patio, ate, and played cards (bid whist) and dominoes. During the course of the evening, when we had begun to wind things down, we all sat at the dining room table and began a deep conversation. The question was raised, "How did you get here in the military?" I can remember getting up from the table and barely paying attention to the conversation as I was putting the fire out, cleaning the grill, throwing away empty cans, cups, and paper plates, and putting away the food. I had attempted to avoid the conversation because I wasn't ready to discuss how I came to be in the military. As the conversation continued, I kept cleaning and trying to be occupied with other "busy work" so that I didn't have to join in the conversation. Finally, everyone turned to me as I was sitting in the living room listening from a distance. "Well, Nick," my friend called to me (my nickname while in the military because we normally called everyone by their last name), "what's your story?"

I sat there for a moment silently, not saying much, and then I said I would prefer not to tell my story, as I could get emotional.

My partner said, "We are all friends, man; if you can't share with us, who can you share with?"

So I reluctantly get up from the couch, entered the dining room, took a seat at the table, and I began to tell my story.

I began by telling the group that after I lost my mother at the young age of ten that my father had remarried and moved us to Louisville, Kentucky. I was eventually kicked out of my house because my father's wife didn't like me, I was forced to live on the streets, get a job, and live from house to house until an elderly woman took me in. I told them that I was in all honors classes in high school, had good grades, planned to go to college on a football scholarship—had even turned down a few schools I wasn't interested in—and how my father wouldn't sign my FAFSA paperwork so that I could get the money to go to college. I told them how his wife hated me and that she was the reason I was treated badly, put out of the house, and eventually that my dad refused to sign the documents or support my dreams of playing football at the collegiate level. I began to tell my friends that it was all her fault, and then—dead silence...

In the middle of my last sentence, I had a revelation and stopped. As tears rolled down my face, my mind began to slowly think about everything I said and all the things that had happened to me over the course of the last ten years. My relationship with my father had deteriorated, he told me not to come home, I lived from house to house and attempted to live on my own and make it in a world with no support. I realized at that moment that my father's wife had *nothing* to do with my relationship with my father; she didn't have anything to do with him not signing the FASFA documents or moving me away from everything I once knew by taking me from Omaha. I began to slowly speak again and say that I was *his* responsibility; she wasn't my mother, but *he was* my father and he should have been the person to take care of me. He should have looked out for my best interest—yet he decided to cut me loose and send me into a cold world without the tools to survive. The room was filled with silence, and I had everyone's undivided attention. All eyes were on me as I stood at the corner of the table with tears streaming down my face and muttering, "I was *his* responsibility—no one could make him not care about me; no one could force him not to care or try to save our father/son relationship!"

That day I began to realize that it was a father's duty, in spite of any situation, to be a father. From that day forward I would tell anyone who would listen that my father had done nothing for me, that he was just someone I lived with for a little while who didn't support my dreams to play college ball, didn't come to any of my sports events, and the church took precedence over his family! My father had done nothing for me, and any success I would have in the future would *not* be because of him, but because I did it on my own…or so I thought…

#StillLearningtheLesson

CHAPTER 31

The Return

• • •

IT HAD BEEN A LITTLE more than five years since the last time I had seen or spoken to my father, and a lot of things had changed in my life. Being stationed in Okinawa, Japan, forced me to grow up and learn about life in general and military life. It was a crash course in adulthood and a culture shock at the same time—learning to communicate off base (young married airmen couldn't live on base), learning to calculate the exchange rate, driving on the left side of the street as opposed to the right, and being far removed from family—these were a few of the adjustments I had to make. For the most part, life was great; I was able to purchase my first car that would actually run without my having to fix or repair daily. I bought a Mazda Luce; I think it was made exclusively for the Japanese islands, because I had never seen one before or after I left the island. I moved into my first apartment, which was off base—and because I was a young airman with nothing, I opted to use "base housing furniture" (this was furniture that was provided to people new to the island who didn't have any furniture).

I was nineteen years old, gainfully employed and learning my new job, working as a baggage handler at the MAC (Military Airlift Command) Terminal. My job at the time was to load bags for military PCS (permanent change of service, or those who were moving from one base to another) moves and space available flights (military members and retirees and their families who were going on vacation and caught flights to different countries). Oftentimes, I would also have to dress in my dress blues and work passenger service (same as a ticket agent when you catch a commercial flight). Everything was falling into place, and I began to become accustomed to military life overseas. I stayed in Japan for five years, six months, and in that time, I went from an airman first class (or two-striper) to a sergeant. I volunteered for an additional three-year tour after the completion of my original three years because I loved the island. I changed jobs and moved to the SAC (Strategic Air Command) Terminal, which allowed me to start my tour of duty over again. After two years on the island, I visited the States when I was twenty-one years old in 1988. During that time in the States, I didn't bother to reach out to my father by visiting or calling. I continued to blame him for many misfortunes in my life and for moving me from everything I knew (Omaha) to Louisville, Kentucky.

In 1991, I started my own family: I had a baby girl, and quickly went from son to father. Although not instantly, my life changed forever as I welcomed my daughter into the world. This same year, I received PCS (permanent change of station) orders from Okinawa to Hickam AFB, Hawaii. This move was like a dream come true—who didn't want to move to Hawaii and live there with all expenses paid! It's normal procedure, or protocol, to take leave en route to your new base. The plan was to fly to Louisville and a stay a week, then drive to Omaha and stay ten days, then return to Louisville and fly to Hawaii to begin my tour.

We arrived in Louisville early one October Saturday morning, and it was time to introduce the little one to family members. Everyone was ecstatic to see the new addition to the family, and we were excited to show her off. My mother-in-law began to inquire as to when I would take the baby to see *my* father, and the response I gave remained an unequivocal "*never*"; I had allowed anger to fuel my thoughts and actions. Eventually, after a few days of badgering, I finally went down to 2401 West Madison. I wasn't exactly sure where my father lived, as he could have moved after six years, and I had failed to inquire, write a letter, call, or ask anyone who may have been familiar, so, I went where I knew he would always be—the Church of the Living God CWFF (Christian Workers for Fellowship). All my life, whenever I needed to contact my father, I knew exactly where to find him. And if he wasn't there, all you had to do was wait on the steps—he would show up sooner or later.

I greeted my father with a halfhearted handshake and hug, and we spoke for a few moments before being interrupted. It was Wednesday night, and everyone knows that Wednesday night is reserved for Bible study. Over the years, I had developed this uneasiness around my father; he was someone I had lost touch with and eventually didn't feel comfortable around. This would be one of the only times in twenty years that I would talk and ride in a car by myself with only my father and me. We left the church and stopped by one of his parishioner's homes (I believe he was the minister of music). We ate, talked for a while, and then departed after an hour. I then invited my father to come and see my daughter. **SHOCKED** As we entered the house, we removed our jackets, and he washed his hands to prepare to hold his granddaughter. As he looked at her, he immediately said, "She looks like Shirley." Shirley was my mother. She had passed fourteen years earlier. Again, we made small talk, and my father decided that he had better get home, so we called it a night.

I eventually departed for Omaha and stayed a little more than a week, and then returned to Louisville for the flight to Hawaii. In the interim, my father called and left several messages on the answering machine. He said, "Marc, this is your dad. We (he and his wife) would like to see the baby." I always felt my father was very fortunate that I allowed him to see her at least once; I refused to subject my kid to the same people who I believed made my life a living hell. So, without so much as a word or return call, I boarded that flight for Hawaii and never looked back!

"Power corrupts, and absolute power corrupts absolutely"—I read that somewhere once. As I looked back on this day, I realized that as I had grown into a man, I'd begun to exercise my "power" as an adult and a father. I used the power to hopefully hurt my father and keep him from seeing my child, all the while hoping to get some type of satisfaction by making him suffer as I had years earlier. Looking back, I think of the Bible verse, "*Do* unto others as you would have them *do* unto you." I had opted to *do* unto others as they had *done* unto me, and it felt good—at that time!

#YoungAndStillLearningtheLessons

CHAPTER 32

Unforgiven

● ● ●

IN 1996, I MOVED FROM Hawaii back to the mainland, as I was to be stationed at Robins AFB, Warner Robins, Georgia. During this time, I had continued to grow and learn from some of my mistakes and missteps. I was the father of a little girl who was also growing by leaps and bounds; she was very active and had a lot of the same traits I had when I was a little boy. She was a natural athlete—she liked to run, jump, play ball, and fight (who knew)! When I found out I was moving to Georgia, I contacted my sister to let her know that I would be moving to the area. She lived in a suburb of Atlanta (Jonesboro) and was more than happy to hear that family would be moving close by. I picked up my car in Oakland, California, and headed east on Highway 80 to Omaha, where I would spend Thanksgiving, Christmas, and New Year's. I experienced the best holiday season in a very long time. My daughter was able to hang out with her cousins, and I became reacquainted with old friends and family.

My arrival date was January 17, 1996 (one day after the federal holiday Martin Luther King Day), and to my surprise, my sister told me that my older brother had also relocated to Atlanta and would also be living with her. My sister and brother-in-law allowed my family and me to live with them until we were able to find a place of our own. Due to some hardships prior to departing Hawaii, I didn't want to live on base at Warner Robins AFB. I felt that Atlanta would be a better fit because of family living in close proximity. I began house hunting in the local area. I had picked up a part-time job at the local Kroger, and I began to save my money in hopes of buying a home, and eventually setting the stage to depart the military someday. Warner Robins was approximately seventy-five miles south of Jonesboro; so it was about a seventy-five-minute ride one way to the base every morning after working at Kroger from 11:00 p.m. to 4:30 a.m. I eventually found a carpool, and we would meet at the local Home Depot off Highway 75 at five o'clock every morning and depart for Warner Robins.

Early one morning I was asleep, and my older brother stuck his head into the room and woke me up. "Marc, Marc…she's dead!"

I replied, "Who?"

"Daddy's wife!"

AWKWARD SILENCE

My father had remarried in 1980 to a graduate student from the University of Wisconsin. She had two children and they moved from Wisconsin to Omaha, and eventually we all relocated to Louisville. I asked what happened, and he wasn't for sure at the time. But he thought that she had a heart attack. We all gathered in the living room and discussed the current events. My sister was in contact with my father to make sure he was OK and that he didn't need any help with arrangements. During our conversations, my father's relationship with me ultimately was questioned by my brother, sister, and brother-in-law. At this time, I didn't wish to discuss my feelings for my father, as I was still very angry and bitter, and just the thought of him brought all these feelings to the surface.

Weeks passed after my father's wife was laid to rest, and my sister planned a trip to visit my father with her family. Prior to her departing, she and my brother-in-law sat and had a few words with me regarding "forgiveness." My father was very sorry about all the things that had happened in the past and wished to speak with me. I was still *very* bitter, angry, hurt, and yes, still dealing with what I call abandonment issues; however, I agree to speak with him by phone. ****FEELING NUMB**** Later that same week, my father was on the phone, speaking to my brother, sister, and the grandchildren. At some point, the phone was passed my way, and I told them to pass it to someone else—I didn't feel like talking. But my sister was persistent. "Hello, Marc, this is your dad. How are you?" I answered with the standard "yes," "no," "I'm doing fine," "the job is fine," and "yes, I like Georgia." And then the moment I dreaded came…

For years I didn't like my father's wife; she (in my mind), was the reason that my father didn't like me, that he put me out, that I couldn't go to college, and that he preferred her kids over his own. I believed that she had brainwashed him into making his kids take a backseat, that we ruined all chances for her to have a husband with two kids and a white picket fence, and the only thing she had to do was trade my sister and me in for a dog, and they would be set...

He went on to say, "I want to apologize for all those things that happened so long ago."

I responded by saying, "Yeah, OK"—with little to no emotion.

He said that he hoped that someday I could find it in my heart to forgive him for those things that tore this family apart, and that he plans to do everything in his power to make it right.

I responded by saying, "It's OK..." and then I hand the phone over to the next person. ***MORE BITTER THAN I WAS THE DAY BEFORE***

My father was *now* reaching out to his children because he was lonely and had nowhere else to turn. I had seen his game, and I knew that if she were alive he would never have apologized; he was only doing this because she had passed on. I could forgive her, because she was watching out for her children. I couldn't forgive him because he failed to do the same. I didn't forgive my father that day. I was still a very bitter young man who was looking at how his life could have turned out, how he was pulled from everything he once knew, moved to a city, and then thrown out like yesterday's garbage. A once promising college career and an education turned into a life of marching and taking orders from complete strangers.

No—I would *not* forgive him; I wanted him to see how it felt to have that shoe placed squarely on his foot. And I hoped it bothered him that I didn't respond.

#StillLearningtheLessons

CHAPTER 33

FORGIVEN

● ● ●

THE ENVELOPE ADDRESSED TO ME had an all-too familiar return address, 2029 Binney Street, Omaha, Nebraska 68110; I anxiously opened the envelope to see what could possibly be coming to me from this address.

The last time I went to church, I was being recognized as a visitor at the church I literally grew up in. My father was the pastor for almost thirty years. It was different finding myself, home on leave from the air force, standing as they recognized visitors. I thought to myself, I'm not a visitor—I have run these aisles, tore up most of these church pews, and fallen asleep on them. I didn't understand why I had to stand. The pastor acknowledged me as one of their own who has returned like the prodigal son. Everyone who hadn't realized who I was now looked in amazement, and the rush of handclaps filled the air; I had left a boy and returned a man...

I opened the envelope and the letter read, "We cordially invite you to a Church of the Living God reunion to be held in October of 2002." The letter went on to say that my father would be the guest speaker for Sunday morning services, and that all the old choir members would be asked to return, along with our old choir director, for a gospel concert on Saturday night and to sing at Sunday morning service. It was signed by the current first lady, who had been a part of that church since I could remember. After all those years attempting to get out of church, I was actually excited to see this invitation. It had been twenty years since we left for Louisville, and I hadn't seen some of those people since I had departed. I immediately responded to the RSVP and started looking for hotels and airline tickets.

Once in the city, I went straight to the church. When I arrived, they were having choir rehearsal. Although I didn't sing any longer, I was anxious to see some of the old friends who may have shown up for such a joyous occasion. I walked in to see some familiar faces, and I heard the familiar songs being rehearsed. This time, there was no sense of urgency like when we were younger. I think everyone took the opportunity to enjoy one another's company and savor the moment, as they were glad to have the chance to do it one more time. My father arrived, along with other ministers, and he did a quick cameo appearance before being carted off to dinner and finally his hotel. At one point, I ended up in the common area with the first lady, and we sat and had an exchange. Sister T had known me all my life: she had watched me grow from a boy, seen me lose my mother, watched a single father raise me, saw my father remarry, and finally now saw me as an adult. We talked for a while, and she finally blurted out, "For a while there, we didn't think you were going to make it to be an adult—we thought the bishop was gonna kill you before you could become a man!" We laughed, and she told me how proud she was to see me grow into the man I had become. She was right—I hadn't realized it, but the odds were stacked against me because I stayed in trouble—or should I say, trouble always seemed to find me!

Saturday night came, and we all dressed and got ready to attend the gospel concert at the church. Choirs came from other churches to celebrate the reunion with us. We had several different groups and choirs sing together again, and they all belonged to our church. Some of those songs I hadn't heard since I was ten or eleven years of age, and they really began to touch me. I sat near the back of the church (my normal spot) all alone, where I had an opportunity to reminisce as the choir sang song after song, and different groups came up and sang a couple of selections. Many of the songs that afternoon were songs my mother requested during her battle with cancer...

Back in the day, my mother would sit at the rear of the church in a reclining chair that was brought in just for her comfort. She was having problems with her back and legs, and this was an attempt to ease those pains. Although she wanted to, she could no longer sit on the hard pews or dish out that discipline an eight-year-old kid such as myself needed. I thought about the times when I was playing tic-tac-toe or clowning with my friends, and my mother would signal for Sister Mary Ann to come and get me. Sister Mary Ann would come and snatch a kid and drag him or her outside and give the kid a little "act right," and then bring the child back into the church. She still makes me flinch till this day...

So I sat in the back pew and the tears began to stream down my face, and they become almost uncontrollable as I listen to song after song that takes me down a very rocky memory lane. Before I knew it the service is ending, and everyone is leaving to find a place to eat and prepare for Sunday services.

Sunday arrives, and I make my way to the church and find my same seat (I never liked to be upfront, so I made it a point to sit at the back of the church). Sunday was more of the same: the choir sang, and the songs began to take me back to a much better place in time and, just like the night before, the tears began to flow again and I couldn't stop them. My father preached that day and, although I don't recall the sermon, I have to be honest—one of the reasons I never went to another church was partially because I had become accustomed to my father's style of preaching; in my mind, many couldn't get the "message" across like he could—they just didn't move me!

So the tears continued to flow and finally, the part heathens really hate— the end of the sermon where the doors of the church are opened. This is the portion of church were the pastor or minister asks anyone who would like to give their lives over to Christ to come forward while he continues to talk about how tomorrow may be too late to try to get your life in order. He tells the story about the young woman who tells her mother that she *almost* went up to the front of the church this particular Sunday morning, but she had some "unfin- ished" business to take care of and she would do it next Sunday. The story goes that she left church that day, and on her way home was killed in a car accident and that she was not fortunate to know The Lord. He said, "Don't delay! You don't have time to get it together, you can't fix it—you need to come to Jesus right now!" The organist is playing, accompanied by the choir (in a very low, surreal manner) that old spiritual, "Come to Jesus, come to Jesus, come to Jesus just now, just now. Come to Jeeesus, come to Jesus just now..."

And before I knew it, I was walking to the front of the church: I had been bitter, angry, and hurt for some twenty years, I hadn't talked to my father on a regular basis in sixteen years, I was thirty-six years old and I still harbored anger from fifteen years old, and it was suddenly time to look that anger in the face and try to let it go. As I walked to the front, the pastor of the church grabbed me and hugged me. See, *everyone* who knew our family knew my story; they saw it unfold, and knew the struggles that had held our family back from being healed.

So when he grabbed me, he knew that I was on the verge of releasing myself from my *self-imposed* bondage. My father and I hugged and talked that day right in the front of the church, and at that moment I was able to release my anger and allow *him* to begin to work in my life! We had come full circle—right back where we started in 1982. It took me twenty years to learn that forgiveness is *not* for the other person; it took me twenty years to recognize and accept the olive branch that my father had extended to me time and time again. It took me twenty years to understand that everything happens for a reason and, although we don't know WHY He chooses us, we must keep the faith that He knew we could handle it.

I believe that I went through my storm at an early age so that I would be a better father and a better man. My sole purpose in life at that time was to be a better father than the one I had. I tried daily to prove that I didn't need my father to be successful in my career and in my life—*not* understanding that all along it was my father who drove me to even want to be successful—a good father, a humanitarian—and looked upon as an all-around good man. It was my earthly father who directly and indirectly influenced me to become the man I am today, and my heavenly Father who kept me when I couldn't keep myself. I finally learned that no matter what happened, it happened in *my life*. *God* is still in control, and if he leads you to it, he will get you through it!

#FinallyLearnedtheLesson

CHAPTER 34

The Circle of Life

● ● ●

IT's VERY RARE THAT MY father visited any of his children. I believe he came to
Atlanta back in 2000 to attend a conference. I was heavily involved with track
and field at the time, and didn't allow my kids (because they were participating) to tag along with my sister to see him and do other family activities for the
weekend he was in town. My father normally talked to my sisters several times
a week and, of course, they would keep me abreast of the goings-on and any
changes that occurred with respect to health and, of course, family gossip. My
sister told me that she and her family were coming up from Fort Lauderdale
to visit because my father had planned to come to Atlanta to visit (she felt this
would be a good time to come up and see my father). I had been working in
Puerto Rico for the past year (2012–2013), and needed to know exact dates
prior to agreeing on a good time to entertain. Because my sister and I both had
stairs in our homes, we felt it wasn't a good idea to have him stay at either of our
homes, so I was put in charge of finding lodging (by me always traveling, I was
the best person to make those arrangements).

My father was scheduled to arrive on a Thursday, as were my sister and
her family. I was still in Puerto Rico, but scheduled to arrive Friday before
noon. My sister from Florida and her family would stay with my sister who lived
in Atlanta, and we planned some family activities for the weekend. Saturday
was dinner at my home. I helped (along with the other adults) prepare dinner,
and we had a few movies playing. Our children attended and actually huddled
around my father, listening to stories or just paying attention while he talked.
My father had this heavy voice that carried a long way, and you could never mistake it for someone else's or act *as if* you didn't hear him when he was speaking.

We finished dinner and hung around in the living room. My father couldn't take a tour of the, as it's a tri-level home, and going up and down the stairs was not something he would be able to do at this time; so he was only able to look at the kitchen, dining room, formal living room, and family room. On several occasions, he mentioned that he was proud that I had been able to obtain what he thought was a nice home and that he wished he were able to look at more. They (my father and stepmother) turned in early, so around 8:00 p.m., it was time for them to head back to the hotel. My sisters would pick them up in the morning and take them to visit other family and friends in the area.

Monday morning everyone was scheduled to work, and since no one else's work schedule was as flexible as I mine, I was elected to be their taxi to the airport. I had planned to pick them up early Monday on my way to work and drop them off at the airport. I arrived at the hotel, and they were waiting in the lobby (old people get up at the crack and are normally ready). I checked them out and got the hotel receipt. My stepmother said that she needed to pay the bill, but I told them not to worry about it—I had already paid. My father needed help getting into the truck; however, he insisted that he would be getting one like mine within the year because he really liked the way it rode. My father sat in the front seat, and anyone who knows Atlanta traffic knows that driving the "speed limit" on the highway doesn't happen. He began to tell me that I drive fast and that maybe I should slow down. ****BLANK STARE**** He went on to say my older sister also drives fast! ****another BLANK STARE****

You have to know my father to understand the irony of the aforementioned statements. I can remember seeing the blue and red lights on several occasions while taking family trips, him calling people names to "get out of the way" and, on top of that, calling them "Sunday drivers" who shouldn't be on the road...

I can recall one trip when we were traveling for a church function along with another church member (who happened to be my mother's cousin), and she and her family were following us in their car. I had to be about seven or eight years young at the time. I can't remember exactly where we were coming from, but we had been "exceeding" the speed limit and the state trooper stopped both cars. I can recall my dad going through the steps and providing the information and documentation. While we were sitting there, my mother was a little irritated. Back in those days, the speed limit was fifty-five miles per hour and you couldn't get anywhere fast. I can remember my father saying that he was in a hurry and that the Lord understands why he had to break the law! My father would also routinely say that you couldn't drive if you had to use your breaks going around a curve. I can still hear his voice saying, "You gotta take that curve, hit the gas, and let him go."

So I found it funny that now this fragile old dude was sitting in the front seat telling me that I drive too fast, and there isn't a fire, so what's the rush. We made it to the airport and I was running later than anticipated. My original thought was to go inside the airport and wait until they went through security, but I had to get going before I was late. Instead, I paid a skycap to take the baggage and get the handicap attendants to come and assist with a wheelchair (they would make certain they made it through security and to the gate in plenty of time). They thanked me for paying the hotel bill and for the ride to the airport. We shook hands and hugged, and then they disappeared into the double sliding doors of the airport. I sat there for a quick moment watching until they were no longer in sight, and then I headed out for work.

As I look back on that moment, I remember the looks on the faces of my children, nieces, and nephews when they were all sitting in the living room with their grandparents talking and my dad telling them stories. I had a chance to see the interaction with grandchild and grandparent, and I began to think of the interaction I once had with my three grandparents (I didn't meet my paternal grandfather, as he passed prior to my birth). I learned that day how important grandparents are, the role they play in the circle of life, and how grandparents bring a story that no one else can tell no matter how much it's written or how much it's passed down from generation to generation. If I were to give my definition of a grandparent, it would be simply three words: understanding, empathetic, and loving (and let's not forget the ones who give you money like my maternal grandfather). You see, they've done their jobs, and they don't and shouldn't have to bear the weight of being the person who raises, disciplines, and becomes the sole provider. They are there to encourage and give that perspective no one ever thought of before because they are wise beyond their years, and no child should be deprived of that experience. For years, I had done just that—deprived my children of really knowing their grandfather because I had a hate-filled heart, failed to understand his role, and failed to be able to forgive.

I learned that I, too, may one day become a grandfather myself and that if I want a relationship with my grandchildren the way I had with my grandparents, it may require me to not only forgive my children, but continue to ask them for forgiveness *even* if I don't think I was wrong. Just as the saying goes, sometimes you have to say I'm sorry even when you didn't do anything you're sorry for.

#FinallyLearnedtheLesson

CHAPTER 35

The Final Time

• • •

I HAD PLANNED TO GO to Native Omaha Days (NOD) 2013. This is where all natives from the city of Omaha, Nebraska, return home for six fun-filled days in the city with everything from gospel concerts, jazz on the green, several beer gardens, clubbing, becoming reacquainted with old friends, and plenty of BBQs. One of the groups I'm in on Facebook, "Proud to Be from North Omaha" (PTBFNO), holds an annual barbecue, and it coincides with the NOD festivities every other year. The week prior to the festivities, I arranged to work in Louisville for a few days and then travel to South Bend, Indiana, to visit a company that I was working with in the area. I would then drive into Chicago (about an hour west of South Bend), spend time with my father's family, and then head to Omaha for the NOD festivities. I normally worked Monday through Friday, with Monday and Friday being my travel days, but, because my father lived in Louisville, I decided that I would depart early Saturday morning, spend the weekend with my father and his wife, and then start work early Monday morning. Driving has always been an awesome way for me to relax and think about things I need to do, a time for reflection and, most of all, an opportunity listen to songs from the new music *I love* to buy. I purchased the new Jay Z album and a few other CDs to keep me company on my one thousand-plus-mile road trip.

I left Atlanta around 3:00 a.m. I have always *hated* to drive during the day; it is absolutely the wrong thing for me to do *if* I want to have a relaxing adventure. (You see, I believe with *all* my heart that I am the only driver who can actually drive—everyone else is just out there to irritate the shit out of me.) I arrived in Louisville about 8:30 a.m. and hung out at the hotel until my room was ready. I then checked in, put my bags away, and went to wash my girl (truck). I, like my father, can't stand to be seen in or ride in a filthy car, so I found a spot that did hand washing and then returned to my room for a nap.

**RING...RING* My cell phone was ringing. "Hello, Marc, this is your dad. Did you make it in, and when are you coming by?" I told him that I had arrived, I just needed a minute to relax, and then I would be over. He told me that the church was having a barbecue and I should come on down and get some food. So I went down to the church and I was introduced to many people, as I was familiar with only a couple of the people in his congregation. I had a good time talking to some and reminiscing with others. At this stage of his life, I can see my father has drastically slowed down. He is losing weight, moving around with the aid of a walker, needs help to stand, and moves very slowly, at best. I observed him and watched his every move, remembering the once big, strong man who instilled fear in my heart. He looked frail, weak, and fragile—almost like a baby who is learning to walk and doesn't stand very well. The barbecue lasts until two or three that afternoon, and we finally depart back to their home, where we sat and talked. My father's wife was sitting behind the computer playing on Facebook. I was also on Facebook via my iPad on the couch, and my father was sitting in his recliner, watching a western on TV. Every now and again, we all made small talk and watched the movie. The next day was Sunday, and I was expected to attend services. So I told my father that I would see him in the morning, and I left to hang out with my friends.

Sunday morning, I arrived at the church and took a seat on the far right side of the sanctuary. The congregation was small, maybe twenty parishioners. My father sat in the pulpit, and most of the time he dozed off, and then he would wake up. He had become the bishop/pastor emeritus, and the younger ministers had stepped to the forefront and were leading. I thought about our days in Omaha, and I recalled how strong and fast my father was *even* as a fifty-two-year-old man; my dad was exactly forty years my senior.

I can remember a particular Wednesday night when I was twelve years old (I remember because it was Prayer Service night), I was supposed to be home no later than 5:30 because bible study started at six o'clock. I was over at a friend's house around the corner talking and having a good time. I was interested in a girl in the neighborhood, so I decided that I would walk her home instead of heading home myself. (Sometimes it's better to ask for forgiveness than permission—or so I thought!) My friend lived in the middle of the block, around the corner from my house on Sahler Street. Back then, this street was a dirt road, and you had to look up to my friend's house from the street. There were two separate staircases: the first was made of brick that went up to the level the house was on, and the second was the stairway to the porch. While facing the house, there was a brick wall at street level that all the kids—and sometimes even the adults—would sit on and talk. There were two ways to get to his house from mine: either I could cut through the alley, or I could go down the street about twenty yards and take a left on Sahler. The alley would come out to my street and was almost directly across the street from my house.

So we jumped off the brick wall, and I began to walk her down Sahler toward her home at the end of the block. The next thing I heard was my father's heavy voice. "Marc, where do you think you're going?" He was standing on the sidewalk in between the corner and my friend's house. Now I know I am in trouble, and I wasn't about to catch a beat down in front of her. So I rolled out—jumping the brick wall onto the hill (no time for the stairs). I ran up that small hill around the left side of the house, down the alley, took a quick left, and headed to the house. Back in the day, I had some pretty good wheels. I was twelve years old, and should have been able to outrun a fifty-two-year-old man who didn't work out, jog, or perform any type of physical activity. I come out of the alley, thinking I was going to head across the street to the station wagon (where my little sister was already in the car) and,—lo and behold—my father was already at the end of the alley in the middle of Thirty-Sixth Street waiting for me! Bent over, with hands on his knees and breathing heavily, he said, "You're lucky I don't have the strength to stomp a mud hole in your behind!" We got in the car and rode to church in silence (while my father continued to breathe heavily).

I looked at my dad to see that he had almost withered away, and I realized that his time in this life was limited. I began to wonder how I would feel when he was no longer here, and how I would act at the funeral. My thoughts were interrupted when the collection plate was passed my way, and I readjusted and focused on the rest of service.

After church, I took my father and stepmother to dinner, and we end up going to O'Charley's. My father thought I was rich, or at least well off, so every opportunity he had and anywhere I took them out to dinner, he *always* opted to order the prime rib, and I had come to expect it. We arrived at the restaurant, and I pulled my father's walker from the backseat of his tan Lincoln Continental. I helped him out of the car by providing a strong, steady arm. We went in and ate, and eventually ended up at the house for another quiet evening of watching westerns and flipping channels. I was there until Tuesday of that week before departing for South Bend, Indiana, and I made certain to stop by and spend a few hours with the old man. I could tell by the look in his eyes that he had enjoyed the company immensely, and I could tell that he was very appreciative for the dinners and lunches we shared for those four days. This was the last time I saw my father alive. I began writing this story today, July 25, 2014, and I last saw my father almost a year ago to the day that I sat down to write this story. We certainly had a very rocky relationship, and I sometimes even thought that the bad times outweighed the good times. But, I learned that no matter the good times or the bad times, we managed to salvage a very important relationship for both father and son. I learned that forgiveness is; always an option and choosing it is a choice; I learned that visiting his home and watching westerns, attending church, and going out to dinner was MY way of giving him his flowers while he was alive; and I learned that everyone makes mistakes, and fatherhood is certainly no different.

..

#FinallyLearnedtheLesson

CHAPTER 36

Heaven, My Home

● ● ●

A FEW MONTHS BEFORE MY father died—on April of 2014—I received a call from the deputy associate administrator. He asked me to take a detail, working as the regional director for the eastern region. We spoke extensively about his expectations of me, and he told me what the job entailed. I eagerly accepted the opportunity to help the agency as it ventured down this new path. The job would require me to be in our Trenton, New Jersey, office a few weeks out of each month, and maybe even more, depending on the business. However, prior to accepting the detail, I made certain to ensure that I would be allowed to keep a few open dates for vacation for my normal visits to Louisville, Kentucky, to spend a few days with my father, and to be able to drive from Louisville to Omaha, Nebraska, to spend time with my family and friends. I was informed that I would be able to keep my scheduled vacation times.

My sisters are the "caregivers" of the family; they talked to one another and checked on my father on a daily basis. I, on the other hand, relied heavily on them to keep me informed of any changes in his health or living conditions. As I began to plan my trip, my nephew called me to see how I was doing and to talk about my father's health. My nephew talked to my father a few times a week, as he was his "spiritual" advisor/pastor as well. I was actually unaware of the close relationship that had developed over the years between my nephew and father, and was *very* pleased to hear that he had continued to keep in touch with him as the years had passed. During our conversation, we decided that we would attempt to meet in Louisville one weekend in July to see how the old man was doing and help with anything he and Ms. Violet needed (Ms. Violet is my stepmother).

I had planned to be in Trenton, New Jersey, for two weeks beginning July 1, over the holiday weekend, due a special project that would require my staff and me to be available during the holidays. The morning started as a normal travel day, with me departing my home at 5:00 a.m. to catch my 7:25 a.m. flight into Philadelphia. As soon as I landed, retrieved my bags, and was in my rental car, I received a phone call from my nephew. "Unc, what's up, man?" **ME:** "Nothing much, what up with you, nephew?" **HIM:** "Making it do what it do."—our normal exchange of pleasantries. He told me that he spoke with Ms. Violet that morning, and things were not looking so good; they were moving the old man back to the hospital because he wasn't eating. I told him that I would be in Trenton for the next two weeks, but we needed to go ahead and arrange to be there as planned. Hopefully, he could hold on long enough for us to see him.

Later, during my drive, my sister called and informed me that she had talked to Ms. Violet as well, and they believed his organs were shutting down and that he was being moved to a hospice at that very moment! We asked how the other was doing (understanding the inevitable was in our midst). She said she was ready and, if he was in pain, then she was ready to let him go. My sister and I have this "thing"; it's unspoken, but how we were raised dictates what we believe to be true as we see our loved ones transition—and someday as we ourselves will transition. We know that death is not a "finality"—it's a *new* beginning. As I was driving, I began to pray and ask for strength. I knew that over the years I was *not* the perfect son, but in recent years, I had attempted to forgive and give flowers to the man I called "Dad."

I arrived in my office and got situated around 11:00 a.m. eastern standard time. Everyone greeted me as I entered the office, and everyone was eager to get me "caught up" with the daily goings-on in the office and region. Anyone who "knows" me, knows that I always have a Bluetooth in my ear, and I am often on the phone conducting business or just talking to friends or relatives—so you never know if I'm addressing you or talking on the phone (LOL). Every day around eleven thirty, those who don't bring their lunch to the office either order lunch or go out to lunch. This day we decided to place orders for pickup and eat in the conference room. Right before departing to go pick up lunch, my phone rang, and I answered it. My sister simply said, "Marc, he's gone..." The only way I could describe how I felt was *pure shock*. You see, all along, my father was the baddest dude I had ever known—he was larger than life to me. Even as a man, he still held that status in my mind that death would never conquer him. So I stood silent for a moment, and my sister said, "Marc, are you OK?"

"Yes, I'm good—my bad." Then I returned the question, "You OK?"

She said she was.

AWKWARD SILENCE

As I prepared to go to lunch, I couldn't help but feel a single tear trickle down my face from each eye. I headed to my office to close the door to allow the news to "sink in." My administrative assistant recognized that something wasn't right and then asked, "Are you OK?"

I said with a smile, "Yeah, I'm good." I closed my door, wiped my tears, said a small prayer, and then headed to lunch. When we returned to eat, the news continued to nag at me. I was certainly still struggling with the idea that he was gone and how I would *never* have an opportunity to say *I love you*, I forgive you, or just sit and talk or listen to unsolicited fatherly advice (LOL). I finally shared with my coworkers that I had lost my father about an hour ago, and it was just now sinking in. I apologized if I seemed distant or inattentive. They all gave their condolences and provided words of encouragement.

Later that evening after work, I kept my normal schedule and decided that I would go on my three-mile interval run/jog/walk. I unpacked my workout gear, dressed, grabbed the iPod, and off I went. No matter how loud the music, I could only think of my father passing and that I would never see him again. Ten minutes into my run the tears finally flowed—I had to let it out. I began to think of ALL the interactions between my father and me: church, early-morning breakfasts, going to his job, football, his second marriage, and even some of the whoopins I had received. Suddenly crying became laughter, and I could only shake my head in disbelief of all the hell I raised and how he had to always get me back in line. So I ran for two hours that day, mostly reminiscing about some of the funny things that had happened over that last forty-seven years of my life, how they had shaped and molded me, and my father's role in it all.

Later on that evening, I went on Facebook and decided that I would mourn differently than most by telling a story, one that I had told many times in the barbershop and to my family and friends. I would celebrate my father's life: he wasn't shot or killed, cancer hadn't claimed his life, and he wasn't in the streets;

he died a man of God—saved, sanctified, and Holy Ghost–filled. Because of where his spirit was most certainly going, perhaps he should be mourning for me and his loved ones who were still here. That day brought me to a place where I could *tell* my story and the story of a man who attempted to live his life the way Christ had ordered us all to. He wasn't a perfect man and he didn't live a perfect life, but as for his children and grandchildren, he was the *perfect* patriarch for our family. He taught us how to live by example—whether good, bad, or indifferent, he was a *man* who stood for something and didn't fall for anything. As a direct result of my Facebook postings, I was encouraged to continue to write my stories and share them with the world. I learned that fatherhood is filled with mistakes, missteps, and imperfect decisions. I learned that if I followed my earthly father's example and allowed my heavenly Father to guide my steps, someday I would see him again.

#FinallyLearnedtheLesson

CHAPTER 37

The PLAN

• • •

ON JULY 11, 2014, MY entire family had gathered in Louisville, Kentucky, to pay our last respects to our husband, father, brother, grandfather, uncle, and cousin at his celebration of life at New Zion Baptist Church. The day started out as a normal morning where we all met for breakfast and began mentally preparing for the day's events. We sat and stood around the lobby of the hotel, reminiscing and introducing one another to new spouses and even some cousins whom we had not met previously. We discussed where we were supposed to meet, the time of the service, and what we would do as a family after all was over. The silver Cadillacs that transported the family to the church were sparkling clean this morning; we could see our reflections in each rim as they pulled in front of the complex. Three daughters and all the grandchildren gathered around the limousines, and one by one, they filed into the vehicles. Flags were placed on each car following the procession, and every driver was instructed to turn on his or her flashers and headlights. I imagine this was to let other drivers and the director (who normally leads the funeral procession in a vehicle with a yellow light attached) know who is part of the funeral.

Once at the church, we had the allotted hour to view the body and mingle. Each person came down the aisle in a single-file line and had an opportunity to take one last look at the man of the hour. As each person departed from the viewing line, they immediately found a family representative they are familiar with and hugged and gave their condolences. This is particularly difficult because I personally had not lived in this city since 1986, and I returned sparingly throughout the years; therefore, some knew me whom I failed to recognize. The mingling continued until five minutes prior to the start of the funeral and, lo and behold, the officiating minister asked the celebrants to please take a seat. He asked the immediate family to exit to the rear of the church so that they may have a final viewing. Prior to entering the church, the family members were paired off to proceed down the middle aisle to view the body and were then seated in the first five rows, which were designated for the family. After the family was seated, the attendants secured the casket, and we were ready to begin services.

My stepmother, Mrs. Violet Nichols, worked diligently to make all the arrangements, and she made certain each family member was made aware of the schedule of events *and* made sure we were fed after the family viewing the day prior. the *plan* included an hour and a half to start and finish the funeral and then drive to the veterans cemetery (which was about a forty-five-minute ride). Because the cemetery works on a time schedule, it was important to *be on time*. So Violet planned to have two songs, the reading of the acknowledgments and resolutions, have the obituary read silently, remarks from ministers (at two minutes each), and the eulogy! The *plan* was going as planned, and each minster kept his remarks at less than two minutes or just barely over. I sat in the second row, and my brother was to my left, my older sister to my right, my other two sisters to the rear of her, and my nephew behind them. Out of the corner of my eye, I could see my nephew stand and walk to the rear of the church as if he was exiting the sanctuary. Then he reappeared to my left at the front of the church as if he was waiting to speak. Now what happened next, I don't have a clue and really don't know how to explain it, but I'm gon' tell it like it happened. He got to the podium and introduced himself: "Good morning. My name is Anthony Louis Nichols II. I am the first and oldest grandson of Bishop Luke Nichols." He went on to say that for much of his life, his father wasn't present, *but* his grandfather stood in for him. He went on to "preach" that he knew whom to go to when things went wrong in his life, how he could always call his grandfather. When his house was out of order, his grandfather told him to go to the Christian store, get some oil, place it on every doorframe (marked as a cross), and speak the words, "In the name of Jesus!" (As the congregation yelled in agreement!)

He continued by saying that not too long after that, the Lord blessed him with a God-fearing wife, one who lifted him up in prayer and prayed with him. The church lit up in a *roar* and the family stood in agreement. He told the story about living in Omaha, Nebraska, and going for his first job interview. At some point during the interview, the man asked if he was any relation to Reverend Nichols. He said, "Yes, he's my grandfather." The man turned the resume facedown and said that his grandfather helped him years ago when he lost his job and needed a place to stay. "I don't need to see your resume—*you're hired!*" Again, the family rose to their feet and applauded. We understood, along with the rest of the congregation, that he would attempt to help anyone in a tough situation! And in closing, he told a story about remembering way back when he was four years old, attended church, and observed his grandfather preaching. He said one day he was at the house, sitting on his grandfather's lap, and he asked him, "Grandfather, how come when you're preaching, you yell a lot?" The following Sunday he preached a sermon entitled "Why I Yell." He went on to explain that when the Spirit hits him, he gets excited, he goes to another place, and he begins to shout and scream about the goodness of the Lord! The congregation went wild, and he walked away from the mic (the organ continued to play, and the entire congregation jumped, shouted, screamed, and danced in the aisles— it was certainly a celebration!

The *plan* was to have a minister deliver the eulogy, and then make our way to the cemetery; however, the *plan* was changed—my nephew delivered the eulogy for my father's funeral. He didn't read a scripture, and he never opened a Bible—he came armed with the memory of a praying grandfather who had helped him at every turn of his life. He spoke from the heart about a man he knew *more* than a pastor, *more* than a bishop, *more* than a father. As the family, we couldn't be more excited to have our own nephew and cousin give the eulogy. Anthony Jr., my deceased brother Anthony Sr.'s son, is a direct reflection of how our father lived his life and, more importantly, how he would have wanted to be remembered.

I've learned that no matter what we plan, *God* still has the ultimate say-so. This was the *best* service I've ever attended; *yes*, I'm biased—but "it is what it is!"

#StillLearningLessons

Epilogue

• • •

A GREAT MANY OF THE memories I have of my father were at 2029 Binney Street, the Church of the Living God, where on many days my father would preach what he would call the unadulterated truth. He would often say that the Word of God had no respect for persons and that he told God that if he wanted him to preach, he would spare no one and tell that truth as long as he lived. On many occasions, my father, during the altar call, would tell the story of how he was saved and how he was called to the ministry.

It was 2:35 a.m. at Seventy-Sixth and Vincennes in Chicago, Illinois, and he had just left the house of a woman (who wasn't his wife) on the way to catch the bus. As he stepped to cross the street, he slipped and almost fell. When he looked up, he saw these bright lights that filled the sky. They were so bright that they almost blinded him. "Well," he thought to himself, "I'll just walk on down here to the next corner, get some of the fellows out of the Seventy-Fifth Street Tavern, and discuss this matter. I want them to see these lights." When he moved, the lights shone so bright that he covered his face. Then he heard the voice say, "You're in the presence of God." His reply was, "God, if this is you, I want you to get me outta this mess." And about two weeks later, he was moving out of Chicago...

He would also like to tell the story of the young woman when he was closing his sermon. He would come out of the pulpit, walk around the church, and tell the story of the young woman who was in church with her mother. After the service, on their way home, the young woman told her mother that she almost went down to the front of the church to be saved. And she went on to tell her mother that she had some things that she had to straighten out first and get her life together before asking God for forgiveness and being saved, promising to do it the following Sunday. He went on to tell the story that the young woman was in a car accident, lost her life, and never made it back to the church the following Sunday. This is when he got loud and said, *"Tomorrow is not promised; you don't have time to get your life right—you can't straighten anything out—you need to come down and give your life to Christ!"* Anyone who was brought up in the church, specifically the black church, knows that during the altar call, the choir is either singing or the music is playing softly. Normally the song is "Come to Jesus's," and when my father was feeling good about the sermon or just good overall, he would always try to sing. Now let's make no mistake—my father was no singer, and he would tell you that he couldn't carry a tune in a duffel bag, but he had this song that he would sing, and the organist and whatever choir was singing all knew the words.

When he finished walking around the church, he would end up behind the pulpit, and he would bellow out, "I'm on the *right road now!*" And the choir would softly repeat, "I'm on the right road now":

Father: I'm on the right road now
Choir: I'm on the right road now
Father: I'm on the right road now
Choir: I'm on the right road now
Father: I'm on the right road now
Choir: I'm on the right road now
Father: I'm on the right road now
Choir: I'm on the right road now
Father: I fixed it up with my Jesus
Choir: Fixed it up with my Jesus
Father: A long time ago
Choir: Looong time agooooo
Father: I'm on the right road now
Choir: I'm on the right road now
Father: He said if I would only live right—did you hear me when I said
Choir: He said if I would only liiiive riiight
Father: He'd make all my enemies
Choir: My enemies
Father/Choir: Leave me alone

Father:	I'm on the right road now
Choir:	I'm on the right road now
Father:	I'm on the right road now
Choir:	I'm on the right road now
Father:	I'm on the right road now
Choir:	I'm on the right road now
Father:	I'm on the right road now
Choir:	I'm on the right road now

As we laid my father to rest Saturday, July 11, 2014, I couldn't help but sing that song in my head as we departed the cemetery. I once told my friends in Okinawa, Japan, that my father never taught me anything and hadn't done anything for me. As I look back over my life and have gotten older, matured, and lived my life as a son and now a father, I can say that those words couldn't be further from the truth. My father taught me how to live life as a *man*, taught me compassion for my fellow man, how to treat everyone with respect and that everyone matters, that service for others was more important than service of self, and most importantly, he taught me about the love of Christ and demonstrated how to live a godly life.

I look at my life and how I live it—my service to others, my compassion, how I speak to others—and even how I have the same effect on others' lives like my father had before me. During my public speaking engagements, I can hear my father speaking, and my coworkers often tease that I go into "preacher mode." I am no longer ashamed of my roots—I come from good stock, and I know that just like my father and his father before him, God has continued to order my steps, and I can proudly say, *I'm on the right road now*!

Acknowledgments

● ● ●

I WOULD FIRST LIKE TO give thanks to God for making this book possible, for without his hand in my hand, I know that this project could never have come to fruition.

I would like to thank my family for putting up with me all these years as I tried to find my way on the long journey to personal peace: **Kelly, Iesha, Joseph, and Gregory Nichols**.

I would like to thank my six siblings for supporting me in this endeavor by reminding me of stories once told, and for making those memories as a family: **Richard, Anthony**, **Michael, Janet, Kathy, and Vicki**.

I would like to thank my aunt, **Ms. Norma Ruth (Walker) Goodwin**, a.k.a. **Grammy G**, who has been my strength, my rock, my mother figure since my mother passed in 1977. She was instrumental in teaching me how to cook and clean, and the one person I never wanted to let down. I attribute any success that I may have in life to you.

Bell Family: Aunt Dorothy, Karin, Della, Collette, and Steve, for your moral support and family history.

Ms. Violet Nichols, for taking care of my father during his most vulnerable time.

Yvette and Byron Nichols, for putting up with me during my teenage years.

Ms. Sherri Brown, who was instrumental in helping me to make this dream come true by keeping it real and honest with her proofreading for accuracy and content. She spent countless hours editing, getting clarification, rereading, making endless phone calls, and providing moral support! Throughout this entire process, you have been my biggest cheerleader and made certain that this was a good product. The format changes you made were awesome, and I could *never* repay you with any amount of money. Thank you, thank you, *thank you*!

I would like to thank my Church of the Living God family: **Bishop Robert Tyler and First Lady Carolyn Tyler,** for everything you have done for me even into manhood; **the White Family (Willie/Beverly)**, always the second parents who I watched from afar. I set my entire life after the path that you blazed. **Sister Rose Jones,** who has known my family since our inception and has provided me with so many encouraging words of wisdom and so much family information that I couldn't get anywhere else. **The Byrd Family (Jimmy/ Brenda),** for continuing to pray for me as I found my way through life's journey.

I would like to also thank my friends for their prayers and encouragement: **Ms. Latrice Howard, Mr. Leroy Adams, Mrs. Vicki Young, Ms. Lesa Evans, Crystal (Arnold) Brown,** and **Mrs. Stephanie Smith Barnes**.

I want to give a *special* shout-out to my Facebook family (bookers and lookers), who have been so encouraging—especially my Proud to Be from North Omaha (PTBFNO) crew, including Angry Alice.

I'd like to give a big, heartfelt *thank you* to all the families who filled in the gaps of my life:

The Ballew Family—The family who allowed me to live in your home and eat your food. You transported me to track and football practice, meets, and games. I have carried what you taught me and attempted to pay it forward. My entire life is a testimony to the investment you made in my life by providing me a place where I could go as refuge for family normalcy.

Nelson Family (Ms. Malita)—For introducing me to track and field and allowing me to go with the family each Saturday to compete. You never treated me any differently than your own boys, and I will never forget what you have done for me.

Trotter Family (Kathy and Cassondra)—I will never forget that booming voice from the stands at track meets and your tireless efforts to ensure that the Midwest Striders family was a well-oiled machine. Your organizational skills were the fabric that I chose to design my team after. I am thankful for you picking me up every Saturday during basketball season as the head coach to play in the Kellom League, and I am grateful that every morning Cassondra would do my sister Vicki's hair before school.

Crowder Family (Debra and Janet)—For taking me in and making me a part of the family when I was at my lowest point in life.

Alexis Family, Stanley Family, Cosby Family, Stevens Family, Murphy Family, Madison Family, Collins Family, Omatayo Family, Christian Family, Frazier Family, and Annette Brown—My *go to* families with the Running Panthers Track Club who made the organization a success...*Boo Yah!*

My first cousins, for sharing your mother with me: John Goodwin, Jimmy Goodwin, Terry Miller, Naomi Goodwin, and Toni Webb.

I would also like to give a *special* shout-out to my **Bryant/Fisher a.k.a. Dozens of Cousins (DOC) Family** for their support and encouraging words of wisdom.

To those I may have missed, please know that your role in my life is not diminished in any way, shape, form, or fashion—please charge it to my head and not my heart!

Marc Nichols

• • •

AFTER THIRTEEN YEARS OF ACTIVE military service in the US Air Force, Marc went on to work in private industry and help start the Running Panthers Track Club of Clayton County, Georgia, Inc. (RPTC), a nonprofit organization that was founded in 1997 with the mission of developing male and female student athletes mentally, spiritually, and physically by teaching them discipline, dedication, and determination. Through his work with the organization as founding parent and head coach for more than fifteen years, he was instrumental in sending more than seventy student athletes to major colleges and universities throughout the United States. He routinely works with the local school system to promote "The Roadmap to Success" program. Marc has mentored local youth and sponsored various students and athletes in the Atlanta, Georgia, and Omaha, Nebraska, areas.

Marc has recently celebrated twenty-five years of service with the US federal government.

He continues to support and encourage youths through various programs in his local community of Atlanta, Georgia, and hometown of North Omaha, Nebraska.

Luke, Janet, Michael, Anthony, Richard, Kathy Shirley

Top Photo: back row Janet Luke Shirley Michael Front row Vicki Kathy Marc
Bottom: Luke, Shirley (holding Marc) Richard, Anthony, Michael, Kathy, Janet

from top to bottom: Luke Shirley Marc Vicki

Luke and Shirley wedding picture

Bottom Michael, Janet, Kathy

Kathy, Michael, Vicki

Luke

Luke

Richard (Ricky), Anthony (Louie), Marc, Vicki

Yvette

Byron

Yolanda

To my FRIEND who has
supported me be it
at work or in my Personal
Life, the WORD friend
is NOT used Lightly and
You my SISTER ARE the
the definition of A True
FriEND.

Thank you for youve support
of my first book and
may GOD continue to Bless

Love
Marc D'Aut

34408789R00085

Made in the USA
Middletown, DE
20 August 2016